GLOBAL MARKET/ MARKETING RESEARCH IN 21ST CENTURY AND BEYOND

Dan Vivek Nathan, MBA, MSc, B.A, FCIM (U.K)

NEWMAN SPRINGS PUBLISHING
320 Broad Street
Red Bank, NJ 07701

First originally published by Newman Springs Publishing 2022

ISBN 978-1-68498-997-3 (Paperback)
ISBN 978-1-68498-999-7 (Hardcover)
ISBN 978-1-68498-998-0 (Digital)

Printed in the United States of America

This book is dedicated to all the (FCIM) fellowship members of The Chartered Institute of Marketing, who tirelessly invested of themselves in Marketing Management.

CONTENTS

Foreword vii
Preface ix

Chapter 1: Importance of Internet, Social Media, and
            Artificial Intelligence (AI) in Global Market/
            Marketing Research 1
Chapter 2: The Role of Big Data, Cloud Computing,
            and Deep Learning or Deep Neural
            Networks (DNN) in Global Market/
            Marketing Research 10
Chapter 3: Global Digital Economy 15
Chapter 4: Merits of Global Digital Economy and
            Future of Globalization and Digitalization 18
Chapter 5: Global Marketplace and Market Categories 24
Chapter 6: Global Market Research 30
Chapter 7: Global Marketing Research 89
Chapter 8: Survey Research: Designing Questionnaire/
            Instrument and Sampling 96
Chapter 9: Sample of Various Questionnaires 103
Chapter 10: Data Analysis in Global Market/Marketing
            Research 127
Chapter 11: Global Market/Marketing Research Survey
            Tips and Analysis Using SPSS Software 132

Glossary 143
References 149
Index 161

FOREWORD

When I was requested by the author to prepare a foreword to *Global Market/Marketing Research in the 21st Century and Beyond*, I was lost in wonder as he was known to me as one of the intellectual calibers of students studying with me during 1970s at the Chartered Institute of Marketing, United Kingdom.

While marketing and business administration have seen many scholarly books and articles emerging on market research and marketing research, we have noticed a dearth of global market/marketing research guides concerning appropriate approaches and software tools for market research and marketing research in the twenty-first century and beyond focused on the global digital economy. No one else has been so exclusively focused on mastering the market/marketing research landscape as a discipline, and few have worked across a spectrum of marketing management communications. The analysis and insights in this book are distinctively competent.

I have been gratified to see this book emerges as one of the best books specifically addressed to global market and marketing research mindsets, approaches, and software tools relevant to global market/marketing research in the twenty-first century and beyond.

This book provides a new platform for marketing managers and business administrators, and I trust it will find a particular place in the field of global market/marketing management, both in market and marketing research management practice and education.

W. Clifford,
Member of The Chartered Institute of Marketing, United Kingdom

PREFACE

Over the past several decades, the world today has been shaped by global economy. The growing economic consolidation of the world points to momentous changes in the organizations/companies of the global economy. Companies in global marketing need to gather information to onset which countries target segments that offer the most appealing opportunities, and to determine how resources should be designated to utilize such potential in the light of the changing market trends. Global market/marketing research circumscribes the complete sequence of marketing research studies that extend across from single-country research at one end to more comprehensive and complex multi-country research studies at the end of the spectrum.

Marketing a product or service globally can be quite a challenge for marketing professionals. The global market/marketing researcher of the twenty-first century and beyond will continue to be transformed by Internet, social media, big data, Cloud computing, Artificial Intelligence (AI), and global economy. The advancement of Internet and communication technology have increased colossal speed of market/marketing intelligence, and this in turn helps to gather data and gets it to the end users for decision-making processes. In other words, global market/marketing researchers are able to learn fast enough about foreign market facts, economic facts, cultural sensitivity, and social facts in the global digital economy.

Global market/marketing research is conducted to facilitate in decision-making in more than one country. Management decisions furnish the basis for the determination of information needs and for the development of research design. Executing global market/marketing research involves numerous interrelated phases—each of which has to be carefully planned, coordinated, and integrated into the management decision-making process.

The first phase in the research process is frequently an assessment of information needs and availability. In other words, the decision-making process facing global market/marketing management furnish the basis for determining information requirements for the conduct of global market/marketing research.

The second phase is decisions on strategy. The management can utilize primary as well as secondary data available. Strategic decisions are based primarily on secondary data. Secondary data can highly be useful in global market/marketing research as it performs a vital function in global market/marketing research.

This is particularly significant in the initial evaluation of marketing opportunities and in locating exact areas for in-depth analysis. It also provides useful ongoing contribution toward forecasting and updating the emergence of new opportunities.

The overall design of global market/marketing research is the unit of analysis. The management will have to decide on the unit of analysis whether they wish to target one country or multi-countries. The sample used can be country-wise. The selection of the unit of analysis provides the framework for creating the market/marketing research plan. Finally, the data gathered through survey is analyzed to furnish some insights into the queries initially posed by the management.

One objective of this book is to provide an extremely compact presentation of the most useful global market/marketing research concepts organized into the essential of research practice. The second objective is to provide a road map to the global market/marketing research process. The guiding principle of this book is to discuss global market/marketing research in the twenty-first century and beyond in the context of global digital economy. Global digital economy has come about through advancement in Internet, social media, Artificial Intelligence (AI), big data, cloud computing technologies with the ensuing expansion of free markets with the well-being of global living standards, consumers' lifestyles, economic efficiency, and unprecedented advancement of technology. In short, advancement of Internet, social media, Artificial Intelligence (AI), deep learning or Deep Neural Networks (DNN), big data, cloud computing, and network of communication systems are the primary forces in the innovation of a single digital global market. The new digital global network is a radical innovation, which fundamentally transformed not only in quantity, but also in quality from the system before it. These technologies have connected the entire globe such that market/marketing information move from one continent to another with amazing ease and speed.

This book is organized into eleven chapters. Chapter 1 covers the importance and need of Internet, social media, and Artificial Intelligence (AI) for global market/marketing research in the global environment as these technologies are constantly transforming the living standards as well as lifestyle of global consumers.

Chapter 2 discusses the current trend—the role of big data, deep learning or Deep Neural Networks (DNN), and cloud computing play a crucial role in market/marketing research. Chapter 3 addresses the global digital economy where trade and industry play an important role in the global market. It is one big entity and is an economic interdependence established among the most meritocratic system of countries such as US, Canada, UK, EU, and Japan that drives the global economic environment and allows the total economic output, movement, and influence of all countries. Chapter 4 examines the merits of global digital economy, future of globalization, and digitalization. It helps culturally which leads to exchanging of ideas and values. In other words, transmissions of ideas, technologies, and values around the globe in such a way as to extend and intensify social relations. There will be an increased flow of communications via Internet/social media and communication technologies. This will allow important information to be shared among consumers and companies around the globe. It will certainly bring the world a lot closer in terms of economic cooperation and trade. Due to technological advancement, there will be an increase in efficiency in all walks of life including companies and institutions. Thereby, all consumers will benefit. There will also be greater ease and speed of transportation of products/services. There will be more investments which, in turn, creates fast economic development among all countries. Chapter 5 focuses on global marketplace and market categories.

Chapters 6 and 7 focus on global market research and global marketing research. Chapter 6 outlines the important role of global market research in global digital economy. It examines each country's market facts, economic, and cultural social facts. Chapter 7 covers the various stages in global marketing research.

Chapters 8 and 9 cover development of market survey research design and sampling. Chapter 8 focuses on designing questionnaire/survey instrument, guidelines for online research, and sampling methods. Chapter 9 identifies different samples of questionnaires in the marketplace. Chapter 10 deals with data preparation and data analysis with different techniques that could be used in global market/marketing survey.

Chapter 11 makes suggestions to use SPSS software for global market/marketing research.

I would like to thank the members of The Chartered Institute of Marketing, United Kingdom, who have contributed to the development of this book. Finally, I am also indebted to senior fellow members (FCIM) of The Chartered Institute of Marketing who have inspired and encouraged me in my professional career.

CHAPTER 1

IMPORTANCE OF INTERNET, SOCIAL MEDIA, AND ARTIFICIAL INTELLIGENCE (AI) IN GLOBAL MARKET/MARKETING RESEARCH

In today's global digital economy, Internet is transforming the configuration of global market by enabling online/e-commerce businesses and communication via mobile/smartphone technology. The unequivocal momentous of the Internet has had on global digital economy is the fact that it has drastically transformed communications among firms/companies around the globe. In other words, it has modernized how businesses work and provided many ways of bringing people and cultures closer together. In short, the Internet furnishes a platform where firms/ companies that are far apart can communicate and share information on products/services. The Internet technology unhooks traditional geographic boundaries for any individual or entrepreneur to access a website from any corner of the globe at any time.

The Internet furnishes a number of advantages for firms/companies willing to expand their businesses in the global market landscape—such as an increase in global awareness, simplified export documentation, access to low-cost market research, and saving cost on communication. The consumers in the global market landscape are endlessly communicating their preferences and opinions through online. In other words, Internet and mobile/smartphone technology allows global market/marketing research to gather consumers' information and their preferences/reactions to products/services. In fact, technology has a profound impact on market/marketing research. The advancement of digital and communication technology is the driving force in transforming global market/marketing research processes. This trend has only enlarged the advent of Internet and social media especially the latter, which is transforming the interactions and communication among consumers around the globe. It has become an authentic and transparent platform for global market/marketing research.

In other words, Internet and social media are swiftly transforming the lifestyle of global society. It is affecting in buying/purchasing decisions, business/firm/company's initiatives in the global marketplace, as well as one-to-one and one-to-many communications and interpersonal relationships. In brief, hundreds/millions of the global population post details about themselves everyday 24/7 via social media. This helps global market/marketing researchers to learn about their preference and opinions about a specific product/service that is available in the global digital landscape. We find the enormous amount of data available to global market/marketing researchers increase with every post/tweet/share. The digitalization has induced an evolution in the way global society communicates. Many market/marketing researchers feel that people seem more comfortable participating in mobile/smartphone/online research if they are able to communicate in ways that feel natural to them. Social media plays an important role for global market/marketing researchers to understand new methods of communication technologies and to adapt global market/marketing research approaches to capture the deepest insights and minds of consumers/customers in the global digital landscape. Global market/marketing research in twenty-first century and beyond will exponentially continue to grow as we move toward innovatively combining new data inputs and developing models that lead to meaningful insights of consumers' mindsets and practical applications.

Internet has a huge implication for global market, and search engines such as Google, Bing, and Yahoo have enabled people in the global digital landscape with the ability to seek anything written that has appeared in the public domain. Satellites to fiber-optic cables and the Internet communications make it free-flowing to have information across the globe. Google analytics furnish webmasters with enormous information about visitors of websites including their languages, pages visited, screen resolutions, etc. The success of the Internet is its architecture, as it's possible for data to flow over different types of networks, so that a message can travel through the wires in a building, into a fiber-optic cable that carries it across a city—even a village—and then to a satellite that sends it to another continent. At the same time, Russia and China have installed technical and legal barriers to prevent their citizens from reaching the global Internet. They have prevented Western companies from entering their digital markets.

Global/world's most Internet users are as follows:

* China
* India
* US
* Brazil
* Russia
* Japan
* Indonesia
* Nigeria
* Mexico
* Germany
* Vietnam
* Philippines
* UK
* Iran
* Turkey

* France
* South Korea
* Egypt
* Italy
* Spain
* Thailand
* Pakistan
* Argentina
* South Africa

Source: International telecommunication (2021)

The Internet's defining feature is that its role and information can cut across geographic boundaries. In short, with Internet of Things (IoT), it can leap out of the laptop/ desktop/smartphone and data center and merge with the rest of the global digital landscape. As people around the globe grow even more attached to their mobile/ smartphones, market/marketing researchers would expect the usage of mobile devices to take surveys to continue to increase. Therefore, market/marketing researchers need to understand the implications of this when designing their surveys. The proposition for designing surveys using mobile/smartphones include: keep the survey brief, use simple types of questions and to evade long questions, avoid images whenever possible, and limit the use of open-ended questions. Today, almost 40 to 70 percent of the entire global population is on the Internet, whereas in the US, the percentage is between seventy to ninety. The role that mobile/smartphones now plays in the lives of many global consumers is one of the most significant trends impacting retailers and brands. Mobile/smartphone features and constant access in the Internet allow shoppers to research, compare, and purchase nearly any product/service from any region of the global digital landscape. Mobile/smartphones have become part and parcel of daily lives of global population. Mobile/smartphones are continuing to evolve rapidly in every continent of the globe—as is the technology for conducting market/marketing research surveys on these devices and the behavior of those utilizing them. Global market/

marketing research surveys are widely increasing as 4G/ 5G smartphones continue to improve, and respondents utilize these devices more habitually.

Globally for many individuals, mobile/smartphone is a preferred platform to communicate rather than a desk or a laptop computer. In fact, it takes about ten to fifteen minutes for surveys on mobile/ smartphone. If a survey exceeds fifteen minutes, the researcher must consider limiting the number of questions asked on mobile/smartphones. Market/marketing researchers must pay special consideration when they introduce themselves via text. Make the invitation engaging. Keep the invitation-text brief, clear, and compelling.

Mobile/smartphone technologies furnish a platform in developing various global market/marketing research solutions to meet marketing management needs. In using mobile/smartphone devices, the speed of response/feedback is quicker and provides the opportunity to conduct rapid-response research surveys in a cost-effective manner. Furthermore, mobile/smartphone research survey offers a promising alternative to derive an overall higher level of survey participation. In short, mobile/smartphone research survey is an interactive research technique in the twenty-first century and beyond, as well as it has the power to reach any part of the global marketplace at any time. As the people of developed and developing countries become more attached to their mobile/smartphone devices, global market/marketing researchers would expect the usage of these devices to take surveys to continue to increase. As such, researchers need to understand the significance of this when designing their research surveys. Researchers must design short simple surveys. They should avoid long grid questions, avoid images whenever possible, and limit the use of open-ended questions. Consumers/customers across the globe are clutching mobile/smartphones and the anytime, anywhere, instant-access capability that these offer.

Consequently, the changing behavior of consumers/customers behind this enormous trend is having a direct, as well as wide-reaching, impact on global market/marketing research. Thus, market/ marketing researchers have incorporated new techniques to guarantee effective "online sampling," and they have also redesigned questionnaires online to make the most of the enhanced features offered by many mobile/smartphone capabilities available in the global digital landscape. The high level of penetration of mobile/smartphones in developed and developing countries, where meritocratic system prevails, means that consumers/customers are transforming drastically fast to online shopping and mobile payments. In fact, they are generating enormous volumes of data—readily available information showing what products/services are seeking via online, what they are buying, and when, where, and for how much they need for products/services.

Over the past decades, the number of hours spent online by adults in United Kingdom has doubled averaging about twenty-one hours per week. In other words, people are exposing themselves to digital and social media. They utilize these technologies for many purposes, including in their roles as consumers as they search for information about products/services, purchase and consume them, and then communicate with other friends/relatives/others about their experiences. This indicates that future marketing among global consumers will largely be carried out in digital settings—social media and mobile/smartphone technologies. It is vital for global market/marketing researchers to examine and understand behavior of consumers in digital environment in the twenty-first century and beyond.

Seventy-five percent to ninety-five percent of the global population own mobile/smartphones. Nowadays, market/marketing researchers use mobile/smartphones as a new research tool to gather data from consumers around the globe. Over the period of two decades, the number of worldwide mobile/smartphone users exceed the number of landline users. The survey via mobile/smartphone can be done anywhere and at any time and are therefore much more advantageous compared to survey via landline phones.

The total global population is about 7.9 billion, and nearly 48.6 percent of the total world population are able to access the Internet according to the *Economist* 2020 report. Seventy percent of Internet access comes from developed countries, and fifty percent come from developing countries. This shows that online/e-commerce trade growth will flourish enormously in the twenty-first century and beyond while the Internet is transforming the global business by leaps and bounds, invigorating online/e-commerce trade across all five continents. The mobile/smartphone communication technologies have grown enormously. Global consumers/customers are constantly communicating their preferences and opinions through different media online. This helps the market/marketing researchers to gather information about their consumers and their reactions to the products/services.

Global communication is directly affected by the process of digitalization of global digital economy and helps to increase business opportunities, remove cultural barriers/sensitivity. The Internet is a vital tool that has added a new scope to global market/marketing research. We find there is an expanding network of online consumer reports that furnish products/service consumer information which are useful for global market/marketing research. Moreover, global databases can be accessed via Internet, particularly global trade statistical data. The Internet world of digital communications has changed the lifestyle of global consumer buying/purchasing power and consumer behavior of countries in the global digital economy. This enlightens the importance of global market/marketing research. The primary factors which impact the global market/marketing research in different countries are namely economic differences, climate differences, cultural differences, racial differences, religious differences, language differences, and historical differences.

Global market/marketing research in social media is the process of collecting qualitative as well as quantitative data from social media platforms to understand social/consumer market trends. For examples to illustrate are Facebook, Twitter, Instagram, LinkedIn, YouTube, etc. They have expanded the digital market landscape in which market research is conducted. Social media allows research to be conducted much faster than traditional surveys in research. It can provide real-time insight into the mind of the consumer. Social media gives global market/marketing research the ability to track current trends as well as emerging trends. Social media furnishes immediate real-time feedback. It can also provide a more detailed view into the consumer. It can predict opinions and behavior. Social media networks are an increasingly vital part of the communication and global market/marketing research. Social media networks are shaping expectations for how consumers communicate, access information, and share opinions on products/services around the globe. Global market/marketing research needs to embrace social media networks and find ways to incorporate them into research methodologies and questionnaire design. Internet and social media are the fastest developing area in global digital landscape, particularly in digital marketing. As people in the global market are even more attached to their mobile/smartphones, market/marketing researchers would anticipate the usage of mobile/smartphones to take surveys to continue to increase.

Artificial Intelligence (AI) uses thousands and millions of pieces of digital data/text to develop a next best action and drive recommendation engines. This insight can be utilized to predict future global consumers' buying behavior patterns, shape/demand/size opportunities to maximize profitable margins. In short, Artificial Intelligence (AI) helps/assists in market forecasting/predicting/analyzing, automation processing, and decision-making. It also helps increasing efficiency of tasks. It also enables global market/marketing researchers to segment the market and tell what motivates the consumers/customers. Artificial Intelligence (AI) can be utilized for issues related to supply chain management. This will reduce the need for human intervention. Artificial Intelligence (AI) is applied to developing and improving models to conduct research, do data mining and predictive analytics, analyze business processes, and predict market trends so forth. There are two types of Artificial Intelligence (AI): Artificial General Intelligence (AI) that can think, plan, and respond like a human and also possess super intelligence. This system would know much of the information that exists and be able to process it at an enormous speed. The second type of Artificial Intelligence (AI) is known as AI-Narrow system that does discrete tasks such as self-driving cars, voice recognition technology, and software that can make medical diagnoses using advanced imaging.

There are numerous applications for drones with Artificial Intelligence (AI) that will make tasks safer and more efficient. Drones are used to physically reach consumers in new and innovative ways. Drones as a hub of technologies integrated with other technologies such as VR/AR, Big data, Cloud, Internet of Things (IoT). Drones are opening path to disruptive ways to gather market to target audiences. When it comes to Internet of Things (IoT), they refer to devices that send data over the Internet. This device could be a smartwatch that sends an individual's heart rate, or it could be a smart power meter that sends a business's power usage. Internet of Things (IoT) sensors are Internet-enabled sending data t and from cloud computing. With analysis of Artificial Intelligence (AI) and Internet of Things (IoT) together with RFID data stream, real-time inventory transparency can be achieved. The advantages of using Artificial Intelligence (AI), it saves time and money for market/marketing research. Artificial Intelligence (AI) embedded in SAS software platform can be utilized in market/marketing research for managing inventory and profitability. Automated Insights (NLG) together with Artificial Intelligence (AI) platform is developing to generate market intelligence reports from global market/marketing analysis derived from data and statistical data. NLG (Automated Insights) translates it into something any layman can read and understand.

CHAPTER 2

THE ROLE OF BIG DATA, CLOUD COMPUTING, AND DEEP LEARNING OR DEEP NEURAL NETWORKS (DNN) IN GLOBAL MARKET/ MARKETING RESEARCH

The world is transforming and extending in a way that consumers could have envisioned two/three decades ago. It is the result of innovation of technology and big data capacities. Big data is the "fuel" of the Internet. It is a well-defined entity from the Internet, although the web makes it much easier to gather and share data. It is the term used to describe how cutting-edge technology will transform how data is delivered to firms/companies around the globe. In other words, it helps firms/companies look for market/marketing intelligence from the data they acquire and utilize this intelligence to progress enormously in the global digital landscape. Big data is a resource and a vital tool for global market/marketing researchers in the twenty-first century and beyond.

Since data is very diverse, it comes from different sources and in different formats—structured and unstructured data. Structured data can be analyzed and processed, utilizing traditional analysis tools and software, whereas unstructured data has no identifiable internal structure.

The amount of data generated 24/7 is enormous. Therefore, there are two options for storing the data: namely, physical solutions and cloud solutions. In other words, these are kind of databases in the digital landscape. However, these databases are not designed for data analysis. It is vital to have a data warehouse to analyze the data stored in databases. In other words, a data warehouse is an additional layer on top of the several databases. It utilizes the data which is located in the related database to facilitate its analysis. Several data warehouses can be created for each department (example: marketing management department, R and D department, logistics department, supply chain management department, and so on) to have its own data warehouse for the analysis of the data. Data Warehouse is an online analytical processing (OLAP) based system.

Big data in global digital landscape refers to the ever-increasing volume, velocity, variety, variability, and complexity of information. It also refers to its challenges, capabilities, and competencies associated with storing and analyzing such huge datasets to support a level of decision-making by marketing management/market/marketing research professionals. In brief, big data refers to the dynamic, huge, and disparate volumes of data gathered by individuals, tools, and machines—both internally as well as externally in a firm/company. The datasets are so large as well as complex that data processing requires new innovative scalable technology. Data gathered must find a pattern in regular or intelligible format/sequence. When it comes to velocity, it is the speed with which data is appearing.

There are two primary reasons for the increased velocity of data—namely, new technologies and amplified amount of information sources. Big data has been introducing new channels of gathering information from consumers/customers/various markets, analyzing and using it in forms and scope. The primary reason for firms/companies to use big data is to facilitate and/or improve the decision-making process. Software widely used for big data processing is "Haddop."

Big data has presented a glut of opportunities for global market/marketing researchers. Big data is transforming the way they do global market/marketing research. Big data can be analyzed computationally even among global population to reveal patterns, trends, and associations relating to human behavior and interactions. It helps firms/companies seek market intelligence from the data and utilize this intelligence to get a business advantage. Over the past decades, big data analysis has emerged to address the limitations in both qualitative and quantitative research methods. Big data can tell global market/marketing researchers exactly how an individual has behaved with accuracy and depth. Big data cannot tell us effectively the motivation behind actions in the way traditional market research methods can. The main advantages that big data introduces is the enhanced knowledge of consumers/customers.

Over several decades ago, market/marketing research professionals were making decisions based upon intuition and experience. Nowadays, their guesses could be confirmed by using data/big data. Market researchers have begun to understand the big data in Microsoft Cloud computing which can be easily accessed by analytical tools. According to Market-Insight report, the market size of big data will grow from $138.9 Billion this year (2020) to $229.4 Billion by 2025.

Future of big data in twenty-first century and beyond

Software for big data will improve and become more diverse.

The volume of data will increase at tremendous rate.

Big data volume and complexity requires extreme speed of analyzing capacity.

The privacy and security are very much required.

Global market/marketing research would benefit enormously from the use of big data information.

Cloud computing is the on-demand availability of computer systems' resource, data storage, and computing power without direct active management by the user. It depends upon sharing of resources to achieve fusion and cost advantages. In other words, the cloud technology's aim is to cut/reduce "costs" and help the users focus on their core business instead of being obstructed by information technology obstacles. Cloud computing has enabled three types of services: namely, software as a service, infrastructure, and platform as a service. These services help firms/companies in market/marketing research. Cloud computing allows companies to focus on their business and react to market conditions quicker. Cloud computing is extensively used for the purpose of storing, computing, and retrieving data.

Internet has reshaped how humans communicate with each other whereas big data marks a transformation in how society processes information. In years to come, big data might change our way of thinking about the world where we live in. Big data will have implications on consumer goods and services, and also it will profoundly change how governments work and alter the nature of politics—even geopolitics. Big data is capable of enhancing global market/marketing research utilizing predictive analytics. Major companies such as Amazon, Walmart, FedEx and UPS and others have large customers' data warehouses.

They use these for market segmentation purpose, and global market/marketing researchers can utilize data mining from these data warehouses to generate consumers'/customers' reports as market segmentation reports and detailed analysis of key trends. This will help for clear decision-making insights by marketing management. The magnification of digital marketing technology has led to an influx in consumers'/customers' data. The research shows 2.5 quintillion bytes of data are being created 24/7 which is skyrocketing with the growth of Internet of Things (IOT). It shows that professionals of market/marketing research understand their consumers better in every respect. They uncover hidden patterns of individual consumer's behavior.

Deep Learning is one of Artificial Intelligence (AI) techniques which is based upon a statistical approach, utilizing data to make inferences based on probabilities. Artificial Intelligence (AI) tries to describe all the features of a man or woman, so that computer could recognize one in an image to feed tens of thousands of man or woman images to an algorithm, so that computer can figure out the relevant patterns for itself. In brief, Deep Learning is a subset of Artificial Intelligence (AI) and Machine Language that continuously analyzes data with logic that is similar to how human brain processes information.

Deep learning is known as deep neural network (DNN). It develops hierarchical artificial neural networks consisting of layers of neurons. In fact, for humans, image recognition and natural language processing (NLP) are easy to deal with. Cloud computing has the capacity for data storage and the computational capabilities. Deep learning or DNN with a huge volume of data can deal with complex functions. DNN has more consecutive layers that are hidden, and more neurons are within each layer. Therefore, this structure allows the neural network to identify higher levels and abstract data features from the raw data. The more complex data features identified by a successive layer are built upon the other. This process makes DNN a thinking machine. In short, deep learning builds up layers of insight to furnish a more accurate/precise view understanding of consumers/customers in the market landscape. Most of the consumers are seeking an omnichannel approach to shopping/marketing, marketing decisions, and purchases via e-commerce/online and offline. This technology tracks the consumers wherever they do shopping.

CHAPTER 3

GLOBAL DIGITAL ECONOMY

Global digital economy is an economy based on digital computing techniques. It is blended with traditional global economy. Today, we see the global digital economy comes of age. The Internet/social media/Artificial Intelligence (AI)/Deep learning/Deep Neural Networks (DNN)/big data/cloud computing have set in progress that has transformed the behavior of consumers/customers in the global digital landscape. Technology, telecommunications, especially mobile communications, media/entertainment, banking/financial sector, retail, R and D in all sectors, and healthcare will continue to reshape through the applications of information technology in the twenty-first century and beyond. In other words, global economic growth and advanced technologies are inextricably merged. The countries of developed and developing countries, particularly countries where a meritocratic system exists, are seeking new ways to cut costs and strive innovation. This is an obvious reason as advanced digital technology drives consumers/customers to demand an efficient use of capital and resources and also education/training, leading to economic growth.

We are living in an interconnected world which would certainly lead to rapid transformation in the global digital landscape in the twenty-first century and beyond. The advanced technology has made developed and developing countries gain access to global capital, talent, and other resources which would allow them to instantly plan for global digital market. Global digital economy is the system of industry and trade around the globe that has developed as the result of digitalization—the way in which economies have been developing to operate together as one system with the utilization of advanced technology. In other words, the economies of the world's individual countries are considered together as a single economic system.

Global digital economy has been picking up so immensely in the past several decades chiefly because of advances in Internet, social media/mobile phones/smartphones, big data, Artificial Intelligence (AI) and cloud computing that have far-reaching implications for the growth in networking global information. Thus, infrastructure of growth in global information network has made it possible for consumers in global digital economy to access global markets and demand the products/services at the best price/quality. In other words, the advancement of Internet and mobile/smartphone technology has been the driving force behind the acceleration toward global digital economy. The advancement in Internet, mobile/smartphone, big data, Artificial Intelligence (AI), and cloud computing not only has caused tremendous explosion of global trade and the creation of global digital market landscape, but also has made it possible to carry different phases of global marketing, with value added in different countries in the global digital economy. Average income in the advanced meritocratic countries such as US, Canada, UK, countries of Europe, and Japan are very high compared to the income earned by the ordinary worker in the developing countries. More than fifty percent of the global households are connected to the Internet. Half of these uses emanate from developing countries.

This is prompting for firms/companies to expand their global market share in global digital economy on a global scale where consumers are waiting for products/services that firms/companies have to offer.

Global digital economy has accelerated enormously in the past several years, mostly due to advancements in computer and communication technologies that have had far-reaching insinuations for the growth in global information network and growth in global markets. In turn, information infrastructure has made it possible for consumers and global businesses to access global markets and demand the products/services at the best price and quality. In short, the advancement in information technology has been the driving force behind speeding up toward a global digital economy.

In global digital economy, *cybersecurity* plays a crucial role as the global digital economy creates a lot of dearth of opportunities for firms/companies in the global digital market landscape. It escalates the threat of breaches in cybersecurity, misuse of IPS (Intellectual Property System), and a reputational damage from open communications on the web, as we find there is an enormous number of mobile/smartphone usage among global population in the global marketplace. This creates risk around the protection of sensitive information such as consumer/customer data.

CHAPTER 4

MERITS OF GLOBAL DIGITAL ECONOMY AND FUTURE OF GLOBALIZATION AND DIGITALIZATION

Global population is experiencing the fourth industrial revolution, so to speak. The advanced computing technology has deeply affected the global economy, and its usage has been linked to global marketplace transformation, improved global living standards/lifestyles, and vigorous global trade. Global digital economy is intertwined with traditional global economy. In other words, it is based on the interconnectedness among global population, businesses/organizations/institutions, and devices that results from the Internet, mobile/smartphones technology, Internet of Things (IoT), Artificial Intelligence (AI), big data and cloud computing. The main components of global digital economy are e-commerce/e-businesses.

Over the past several years, there is a tremendous growth in computing technologies. When it comes to merits of global digital economy, companies such as Google, Microsoft, Apple, Amazon, and Airbus have transformed the digital economy on a global level. In short, the advancement of technologies has significantly transformed manufacturing, marketing, market/marketing research, logistics, supply chain, etc. and lowered the cost of doing business. It has increased job opportunities and strengthened global economic growth. The higher economic growth and fast adoption of digitalization in developing countries is putting their consumers/customers at the center of companies' growth strategies, and we are seeing the rise of the sharing economy, blockchain technology, and change in manufacturing driven 3D/4D printing. The "sharing economy" means people/organizations connect online/Internet to share products/services. "Blockchain" means digital/computerized digital ledger technology that tracks transactions. Another example of blockchain technology is Bitcoin. The global digital economy relies on personal/consumer data collection. These big data have an economic value in twenty-first century and beyond.

When platform compile personal/consumer data, they gather consumer/customer preference and interests on products/services. These gathered data allow firms/companies to set in motion targeted action on the consumers/customers. Algorithms classify reference and prioritize the preferences of consumers/customers to better predict their behavior.

Doing business across the world is known as "global business" whereas "global digital economy" is advocated by the economically advanced nations especially countries of *meritocratic system* to free up trade across the globe communicating through advanced digital technologies. Let us differentiate the *meritocratic system* and *monocratic system* that prevails in the world. *Meritocratic system* is the only system that creates opportunities for everyone, including the most vulnerable. This system articulates the power of *free markets* and individual *freedom* in unleashing what human creativity can accomplish in a *free-market economy*; whereas the *monocratic system* is a system of *autocracy/authoritarianism/totalitarianism*. These are characterized by having a single dominant ruler who may use force and the repression of individual rights to maintain power.

Five decades ago, globalization has quickly triggered the global development that results in extensive and overwhelmingly changed in economic and environment. Globalization has been a force for dramatic change in different countries of five continents. What is globalization? Globalization refers to the growing integration of the world, coupling together into one global economy. In short, global economy is the collective term of individual country's economy whereas globalization basically means business operating at global landscape. As a result of globalization, the world has become a smaller place, and the interactions among people with different cultures have increased.

Global digital economy has come about through advanced Internet/social media technologies with the consequent expansion of free markets, rising global living standards, lifestyles, economic efficiency, individual freedom, and democracy. In other words, advancement in digital computer technology and communication systems are the main sources in the creation of a single global market. Internet and social media have connected the entire globe through such information, instantaneous news, and money transactions that move from one country to another continue with astonishing ease and speed. The network, via Internet/mobile technology, is also creating a global market in any product/service as well as in culture/religion.

The most promising linkage for global digital economy is the global transfer of knowledge and ideas. As digitalization occurs, new knowledge and ideas are integrated into the global digital economy which leads to a technological fourth industrial revolution. The contribution of digitalization to ideas and knowledge transfer is an important factor in the contribution of global digital economy to economic change. We find that communication via Internet and social media makes informational flow across natural boundaries. It has been customary to appraise economic globalization in terms of global flows of trade and capital. As global trade and capital movements increase, as people of different countries of five continents migrate, and as information via Internet and social media is spread, the global digital economy becomes more integrated and ultimately globalized, and in turn, global digital economy is vital for economic, social, and cultural dimensions. In short, increased integration has strong implications for the performance of the global digital economy. Until the twenty-first century, global economy dominated by the meritocratic system prevailed in countries such as US, UK, Canada, EU, and Japan. New patterns of global digital economy have been emerged toward rapid development in other parts of the world. The digitalization of marketing/digital marketing management, automation, production skills, dissemination through investment of different countries, human migration, and education play a vital role.

In brief, global digital economy is an economic process of interaction and integration that is associated with sociocultural aspects in global market economy through digital technologies. It has been advanced due to communication technology. It provides greater access to state-of-the-art technology and business practices around the globe. Digitalization and state-of-the-art technology have changed the environmental, socioeconomic, and cultural elements of the world. In other words, globalization and state-of-the-art technology have made it easier to see people on the other region of the globe as a neighbor instead of a stranger.

The future of global digital economy and digitalization

Trade is becoming more focused on specific regions in the European Union and Asia. That is, to some extent, the result of greater domestic demand from emerging market countries, but it is also being driven by the increased importance of ease and speed. In global digital economy, an asymmetrical amount of time and money resources will be spent on Internet/online. In global digital economy, money is equivalent to cryptocurrencies (Bitcoin) in years to come. Digital assets such as "unique context," "digital codes," and "digital art" have an assigned value in the global digital landscape. Digital money will be adopted as units of exchange. In brief, a robust global digital economy will form around "digital assets." In terms of digitalization, Artificial Intelligence (AI), together with deep learning or deep neural networks (DNN), will become the norm in global market/marketing research because of its increasingly accurate ability to analyze consumer/customer behavior and feed into better, more interactive purchasing experience.

Middle-income countries such as Brazil, Mexico, and South Africa will benefit from the global digital economy. These countries also have enormous opportunities to benefit from digitalization by adopting them by building them. The rise of digitalization means firms/companies don't have to worry as much about the cost of labor when choosing where to make investments. In years to come, trade in services will take up a greater share of the global digital economy as manufacturers and retailers introduce new ways of providing services. Mobile Internet, digital payments, e-commerce, online financial services tend to contribute more inclusive growth.

The enormous increase and growth of Internet connectivity, social media, and Artificial Intelligence (AI) are also transforming trading patterns around the globe. In other words, the availability of inexpensive fast digital communication technology has raised up trade. The Internet of Things (IOT) with Internet connection keep informed of shipments arouse the globe and monitor their supply chains. Moreover, e-commerce platforms allow buyers and sellers to find each other more easily. The technical advancement in Artificial Intelligence (AI) powered vision, robotics in manufacturing-automation, and 3D printing play an important role in global digital economy. The immense increase growth in automation means firms/companies don't have to agonize as much about the labor cost when choosing where to invest.

Many firms/companies are setting up fully automated factories to make products such as clothes/textiles, shoes, toys—even automobiles.

For the past decade, global trade in service has accelerated more than 60 percent faster than global trade in products/goods. 5G wireless networks will give firms/companies new ways to deliver services. New technology will let firms/companies remotely deliver more services, especially for education and health care. The countries of meritocratic systems that specialize in exporting services such as US, UK, France, Netherlands, and Singapore are in a good position to turn to account on these trends. Furthermore, cloud computing has played a vital role in pay-as-you-go and subscription models for storage and software, freeing users from making heavy investment in their own hardware.

When global market/marketing researchers analyze the demographic structure of a country, they find that demographic structure shapes the country's integration into the global workforce. The shortage of workforce is an incentive to develop of labor-saving technologies and to promote digitalization.

Consequently, this trend reduces the costs of global trade which in turn accelerates global digital economy.

Global digital economy, in terms of "digitalization/digital transformation," online/e-commerce, is flourishing so swiftly as an outgrowth of global consumers have already spent almost four trillion dollars in 2019. This trend has continued to grow across all five continents to give access to products/services. The penetration rate of buying/purchasing power of consumers globally is 47 percent.

CHAPTER 5

GLOBAL MARKETPLACE AND MARKET CATEGORIES

Global marketplace is the total of all consumers across the globe who want/need or might want/need your products/services. Global marketplace is not limited to specific geographic locations, but rather involves the exchange of goods/services anywhere in the world, so that consumers and businesses have the access to the products/services around the globe.

Global marketing encounters problems that are considerably more complex than those encountered in relation to domestic marketing. Global marketing in different countries is complex by the diversity of environments in which marketing operations are conducted. In other words, countries and cultures differ about socioeconomic conditions among population, and also levels of literacy rate vary among countries. Language/linguistics and religious affiliations are also another factor adding to the complexity of global markets. Language is only the most obvious impediment to overcome when conducting global market/marketing research in a foreign culture. Global market/marketing researchers must anticipate differences in lifestyles and family structures, economic systems, as well as shopping/consumers habits to achieve an optimum research survey result.

There are four stages: namely, planning, managing the survey project, selection of translators/modulators, and interpretation of findings/results. Different communications and transportation available vary from one country to another. Global marketing thus entails marketing operation in a diverse and intricate environment, and it requires extensive global market/marketing research in order to acquire familiarity with the environment. Global market/marketing research provides information about the environment and generates increased understanding and ability to cope effectively with complexities and also prevents global marketing management making errors by failing to adapt strategy and moves to different environment they encounter.

Secondary research is adequately enough for the information on different markets. Global market/marketing researchers utilize secondary data as a starting point to gather information on global markets. Secondary market research furnishes guidance to the researchers by pointing out the gaps in the information that is available in order to find inconsistencies that can be addressed with the use of primary research data. There is enormous secondary data on global markets available for global market/marketing researchers. Therefore, global market/marketing researchers have got to conduct thorough research for secondary data sources in areas of interest and use data that is relevant to their global market/marketing research.

When it comes to market categories, we find there are two categories of systems in the world: namely, meritocratic system and monocratic system. The meritocratic system has developed incrementally in the Western countries over the past two centuries—namely US, UK, Canada, European countries, and Japan—and the monocratic system that is exemplified by China, but also exists in other parts of Asia—for example, North Korea/DPRK, Vietnam etc., and parts of Europe—for example, Russia and Central Asia, and Latin America—for example in Cuba.

In Western European countries and in North America and a number of other countries such as India, Indonesia, and Japan, meritocratic systems of economy dominate. This type of system concentrates the vast majority of production in the private sector of the economy. A meritocratic system of economy allows and encourages talent to rise and tries to guarantee opportunities for all through measures such as free schooling and inheritance taxes, whereas monocratic system privileges high economic growth and limits individual political and civic rights.

The global/world's largest companies by market capitalization operate within a range of different market sectors—namely, technology, communications, energy, consumer cyclicals, and financial services. The market capitalization is calculated by multiplying the total number of its shares outstanding by the current market price of a single share. For example, the technology market sector is the category of stocks relating to the R and D/distribution of technologically-based goods and services. The technology sector contains companies revolving around the manufacturing of electronics, creation of software, computers/products/services relating information technology. When it comes to energy market sector, it comprises companies engaged in exploration and production, refining and marketing, and storage and transporting of oil/gas and coal and consumable fuels. The energy sector also includes companies that offer oil and gas equipment and services.

The global/world's largest companies (2021) are as follows:

United States of America

> Walmart (US)
> Amazon (US)
> CVS Health (US)
> Berkshire Hathaway (US)
> McKesson (US)
> Ameri source B (US)
> Alphabet (US)
> Exxon (US)
> AT & T (US)
> Costco Wholesale (US)

Cigna (US)
Cardinal Health (US)
Microsoft (U.S)
Walgreen Boots Alliance (US)
Kroger (US)
Home Depot (US)
JP Morgan Chase (US)
Verizon Communications (US)
Ford Motor (US)
General Motors (US)
Anthem (US)
Centene (US)
Fannie Mae (US)
Comcast (US)
Chevron (US)
Dell Technologies (US)
Bank of America (US)
Target (US)
Lowe's (US)
Marathon Petroleum (US)
Citigroup (US)
Facebook (US)
UPS (US)
Johnson & Johnson (US)

Source: *Fortune* (2021)

Other parts of the world

Toyota Motor (Japan)
Volkswagen (Germany)
Samsung Electronics (South Korea)
BP (UK)
Royal Dutch Shell (Netherlands)
Daimler (Germany)
Trafigura (Singapore)

Glencore (Switzerland)
Aliany (Germany)
AXA (France)
Honda Motor (Japan)
Mitsubishi (Japan)
Total Energies (France)
Deutsche Telekom (Germany)
BMW (Germany)
Nippon Telegraph & Telephone (Japan)
Japan Post Holdings (Japan)
Itochu (Japan)
Assicurazioni General (Italy)
Nestle (Switzerland)
Hyundai Motor (South Korea)
Royal Ahold Delhaize (Netherlands)
Sony (Japan)
Credit Agricola (France)
BNP Paribas (France)
Bosch Group (Germany)
Tesco (UK)
AEON (Japan)

Source: *Fortune* (2021)

In the twenty-first century, more than 90 percent of all trade is seaborne. This shows that global industrial production has vital importance of seaports in the global supply chain. Even logistics and marketing play a crucial role.

Global/world's busiest ports that deal with marketing/supply chain/logistics are as follows:

Shanghai (China)
Singapore
Ningbo, Zhoushan (China)
Shenzhen (China)

Guangzhou (China)
Busan (South Korea)
Qingdao (China)
Hong Kong (China)
Tianjin (China)
Rotterdam (Netherlands)
Dubai (UAE)
Port Klang (Malaysia)
Antwerp (Belgium)
Xiamen (China)
Kaohsiung (Taiwan)
Los Angeles (US)
Hamburg (Germany)
Tanjung Pelepas (Malaysia)
Dalian (China)
Laem Chabang (Thailand)

Source: Lloyd's (2021)

CHAPTER 6

GLOBAL MARKET RESEARCH

Global market research is the task of finding out what consumers/ customers want and planning to fulfill their needs. Global population today is immeasurably digital using Internet, mobile/smartphones, linking consumers/customers around all five continents. With the huge amount of information consumers/customers are exposed to, it becomes mandatory for global market/marketing researchers to understand their behavior/emotions/preferences/opinions and decision-making patterns.

The secondary data plays an important role in global market research. Gathering secondary data in global market/marketing research often furnishes an important input for strategic decisions relating to initial market entry, market share, expansion, and change in market environmental conditions. The initial stage of the global market research involves desk research based on secondary data available in each country's updated statistical data currently available from various sources, including respective government—statistics, economic, and social statistics, demographic data publications from industry and trade associations. Secondary data are relatively inexpensive to collect in global market/marketing research process.

The sources of secondary data provide an easy means of rapidly gaining some initial awareness of the market environment in a particular country. The secondary data are used initially to identify potential concerns that merit an in-depth investigation based on initial research. In other words, the secondary data performs a vital function in the global market/marketing research, and this is particularly significant in the initial evaluation to pinpoint key areas for in-depth study and also for adaptation of marketing strategy.

To take advantage of global market aspects, global market/marketing researchers must know each country's top issues such as *market facts*, including population, age structure, language, and literary rate; *economic prospects*, including principal exports, main export destinations, principal imports, main origin of imports, GDP, purchasing power index, economic freedom index, structural employment rate, structure of employment—service sector, industrial sector and agricultural sector; and *cultural social facts*, including number of households, average number of households, religion, Internet usage, and Internet penetration.

Comparison of percentage of Internet access and Internet penetration among countries of meritocratic system and monocratic system

Country	Internet Access	Internet Penetration
US	75.2	89.8
Canada	92.7	94.0
Mexico	63.9	66.5
China	54.3	59.3
Russia	76.0	6.1
Vietnam	49.6	70.4
UK	94.6	94.2
France	80.5	92.3
Germany	84.4	96.0
Ireland	84.5	91.9

Italy	61.3	92.5
Netherlands	93.2	95.6
Japan	90.9	93.5
South Korea	95.1	95.9
India	34.5	40.9
Pakistan	15.5	32.4
Singapore	84.4	88.4
Indonesia	32.3	63.5
Malaysia	80.1	81.4
Australia	86.5	87.8
New Zealand	90.8	90.8
Israel	81.6	78.5
Egypt	45.0	48.1
Brazil	67.5	70.1
Chile	82.3	92.4
Cuba	49.1	
Venezuela	64.3	83.0
Syria	34.2	32.6

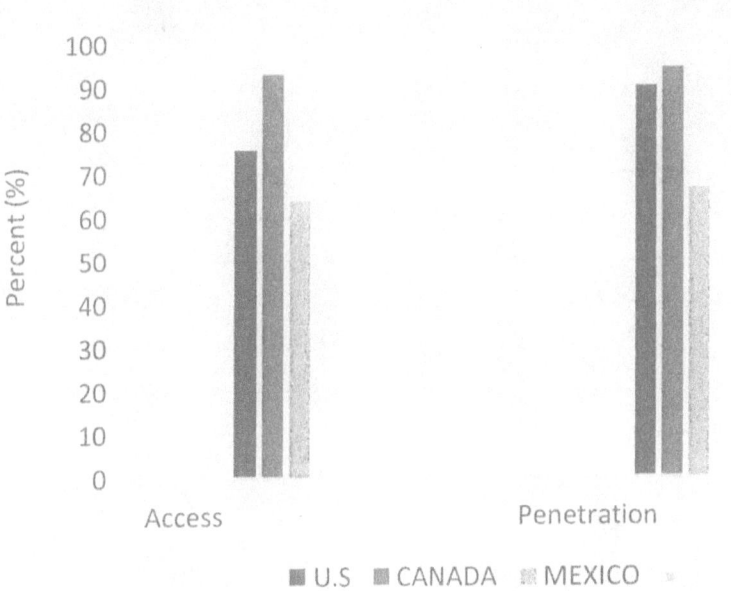

NORTH AMERICA: Internet Access & Internet Penetration

Source : EIU-2020 Statistics

EUROPE:Percentage of Internet Access & Internet Penetration

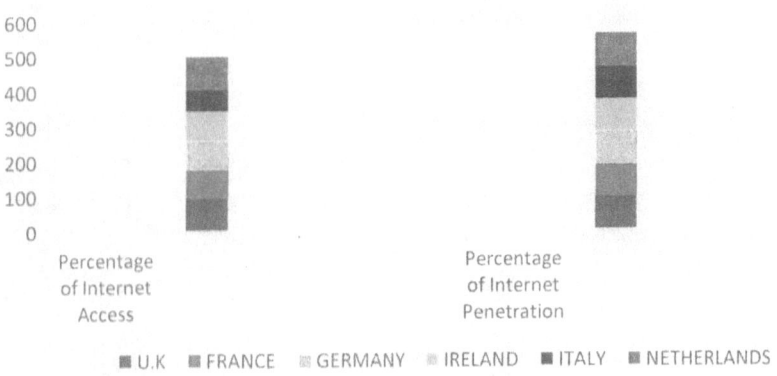

U.K   FRANCE   GERMANY   IRELAND   ITALY   NETHERLANDS

Source : EIU - 2020 - Statistics

ASIA:Internet Access & Penetration

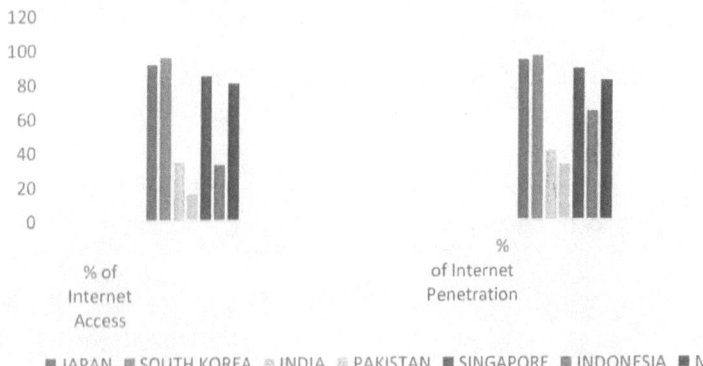

JAPAN   SOUTH KOREA   INDIA   PAKISTAN   SINGAPORE   INDONESIA   MALAYSIA

Source : EIU - 2020- Statistics

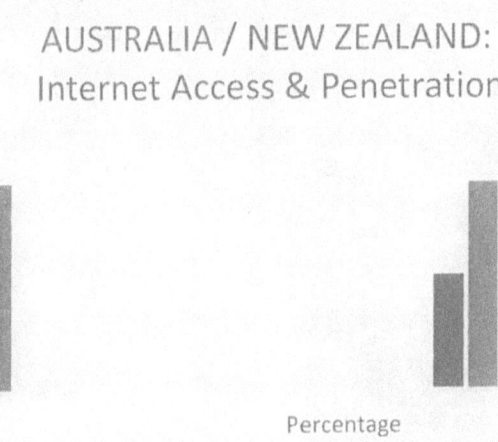

AUSTRALIA / NEW ZEALAND:
Internet Access & Penetration

Source : EIU – 2020 – Statistics

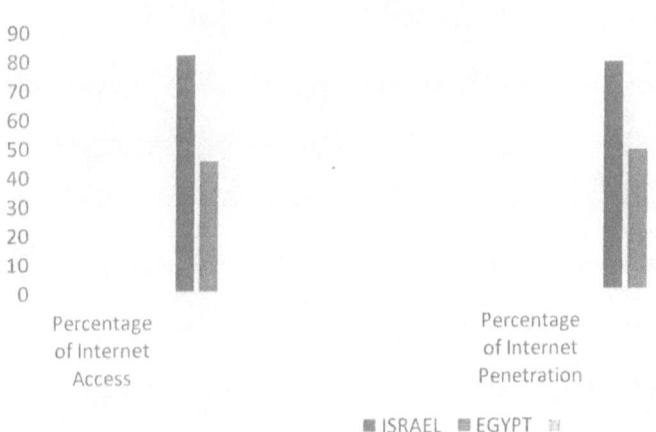

MIDDLE EAST: Internet Access & Penetration

Source : EIU – 2020 – Statistics

SOUTH AMERICA: Internet Access & Penetration

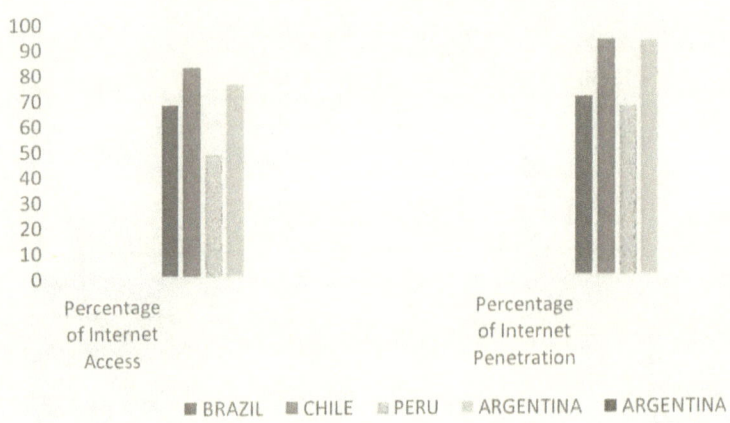

Source : EIU - 2020 - Statistics

COUNTRIES OF MONOCRATIC SYSTEM : Percentage of Internet Access & Penetration [Latest Data]

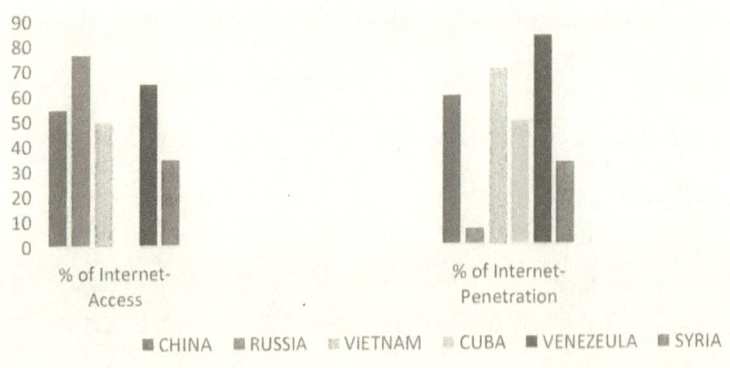

Source : EIU - 2020 -Statistics

Source: EIU (2021) Statistics
Argentina   75.8   92.0
Source: EIU (2021) Statistics

COUNTRIES OF MERITOCRATIC SYSTEM

United States of America

Market facts:
Population: 334,998,398 (2021)
Age structure: <14 = 19%; 15–24 = 14%; 25–54 = 40%; 55–64 = 13%; 65> = 15%
Language: English, Spanish, Other Indo-European, Asian/Pacific Island
Literacy rate: 99.0%

Economic prospects:
Principal export: capital goods (excluding vehicles), industrial supplies, consumer goods (excluding vehicles), vehicles and products
Main export destinations: Canada, Mexico, China, Japan, EU
Principal import: industrial supplies, capital goods (excluding vehicles), consumer goods (excluding vehicles), vehicles and products
Main origins of imports: China, Canada, Mexico, Japan, EU
GDP: $63,544 per head
Purchasing Power Index: 89.8 (2019)
Economic freedom index: 76.8
Structure of employment:
    Service sector: 79.1%
    Industrial sector: 19.4 %
    Agricultural sector: 1.4 %
Structural employment rate (Ages 15–64): 70.7 (2018)

Cultural social facts:
Number of households: (m) 126.1
Average number per households: 2.6
Religion:
    Christians: 78.3%,
    Nonreligious: 16.4%
    Other: 2.0%
        Jewish: 1.8%
        Muslims: 0.9%
        Hindus-:0.6%
Internet usage: 313,322,868 (2019)
Internet penetration: 89.8%

The US is culturally diverse with many ethnicities and has immigrants from all continents of the globe, with the majority of the people being of European descent. Until 1840, immigrants came mostly from England and Scotland, but thereafter increasing from other—mainly European—lands including Ireland, Germany, Sweden, Norway; and from the 1860s, Italy and Slavic countries. From 1965, large numbers of Latinos/Hispanics, and Asians. The first black came as slaves in 1619. The majority of them live in the South and large cities like Chicago, Washington, D.C., and Michigan.

The minorities include Latinos/Hispanics from South and Central America, African Americans from Africa and West Indies, and Asians from Far East and India. The majority of the population live in urban areas. There are four regions in the US and fifty states, with each having its own nuances and social norms, and there are many regional differences in terms of dialect and colloquial behavior.

Though most Americans identify themselves as middle class, American society and its culture are considerably fragmented. Social class, generally described as a combination of educational attainment, income, and occupational prestige, is one of the greatest cultural influences in US. Nearly all cultural aspects of mundane interactions and consumer behavior in the US are guided by a person's location within the country's social structure. Distinct lifestyles, consumption patterns, and value are associated with different classes. In the US, occupation is one of the prime factors of social class and is closely linked to an individual's identity.

Greetings tend to be more formal and come with a handshake. They are friendly. They are often quickly on a first-name basis, so to be prepared for them to share their first name and yours. They greet with a firm handshake while making eye contact.

Canada

Market facts:
Population: 37,943,231 (2021)
Age structure: < 14 = 16%; 15–24 = 13%; 25–54 = 41%; 55–64 = 14%; 65> = 7%
Language: English, French
Literacy rate: 99.0%

Economic facts:
Principal export: energy products, motor vehicles and parts, metal and mineral products, consumer goods
Main export destinations: United States, China, United Kingdom, Japan, EU
Principal import: consumer goods, motor vehicle and parts, electronic and electrical equipment, energy products
Main origins of imports: United States, China, Mexico, Japan, EU
GDP per head: $51,210
Purchasing Power Index: 95.9
Economic Freedom Index: 77.7
Structure of employment:
    Service sector: 79.0%
    Industrial sector: 19.5%
    Agricultural sector: 1.5%
Structure of employment rate: (Ages 15–64): 73.8 (2018)

Cultural social facts:
Number of households: 14.1 (m)
Average number per households: 2.6

Religion:
  Christians: 69.0%,
  Nonreligious: 23.7%
  Other: 2.8%
    Muslims: 2.1%
    Hindus: 1.4%
    Jewish: 1.0%
Internet usage: 35,742,154 (2020)
Internet penetration: 94.0%

Canada has twelve provinces/territories. Diversity exists. The population is predominantly of British and French stock, though it includes many Germans, Italians, Ukrainians, Dutch, and other origins and Indians and Inuit (Eskimos). Of the total population, majority speak English, and the other language they speak is French. The most populous provinces being Ontario, Quebec, British Columbia. The largest urban areas are Toronto, Montreal, Vancouver, Ottawa, Edmonton, Calgary, and Winnipeg.

Canadians are known to be some of the most polite, tactful, and peace-loving people. It is difficult to specify any national traits in terms of communication in Canada due to its regionalism and cultural diversity. However, businesspeople are generally polite and easygoing. Arrive to business meetings on time—it's important. Shake the hands of the person meeting you. Equality of the sexes is important. Avoid talking about politics, religion, and money.

Mexico

Market facts:
Population: 132,328,035 (2021)
Age structure: < 14 =28%; 15–24 = 18%; 25–54 = 41%; 55–64 = 7%; 65> = 18%
Language: Spanish, Indigenous language
Literacy rate: 94.9%

Economic facts:

Principal exports: manufactured goods, crude oil and products, agricultural products, mining products

Main export destinations: United States, Canada, Spain, China

Principal imports: intermediate goods, consumer goods, capital goods

Main origins of imports: United States, China, Japan, South Korea

GDP per head: $18,333

Purchasing Power Index: 41.8

Economic Freedom Index: 64.7 (2019)

Structure of employment:

    Service sector: 61.1%

    Industrial sector: 26.1%

    Agricultural sector: 13.0%

Structure of employment rate: (Ages 15–64): 61.5 (2018)

Cultural social facts:

Number of households: (m) 33.8

Average number per household: 3.8

Religion:

Christians: 95.1%,

    Nonreligious: 4.7%

    Hindus: <0.1%

    Jewish: <0.1%

    Muslims: <0.1%

    Other: <0.1%

Internet usage: 88,000,000 (2019)

Internet penetration: 66.5%

Majority live in the towns and cities of larger being Mexico City, the capital. Guadalajara is the second largest city. More than 60 percent of Mexicans are mestizos (mixed Indians and white stock). The culture of an individual Mexican is influenced by their familial ties, gender, religion, location, and social class, among other factors. They are seen to be friendly and hospitable people. Their attitude and behavior tend to be a blend of Native Indian and European (white).

Mexicans emphasize hierarchical relationships. People respect authority and look to those above them for guidance and decision-making.

United Kingdom

Market facts:
Population: 67,886,011 (2021)
Age structure: <14 = 18%; 15–24 = 13%; 25–54 = 41%; 55–64 = 12%; 65> = 18%
Language: English, Scots, Scottish Gaelic, Welsh, Irish
Literacy rate: 99.0%

Economic facts:
Principal exports: machinery and transport equipment, chemicals and related products, mineral fuels and lubricants, food, drink and tobacco
Main export destinations: Germany, United States, Netherlands, France, EU
Principal imports: machinery and transports equipment, mineral fuels and lubricants, chemicals and related products, food, drink and tobacco
Main origins of imports: Germany, China, Netherlands, France, EU
Purchasing Power Index: 94.2
Economic Freedom Index: 78.9 (2019)
Structure of employment:
  Service sector: 80.7%
  Industrial sector: 18.1
  Agricultural sector: 1.1%
Structure of employment rate (Ages 15–64): 75.0 (2018)
GDP per head: $44,916

Cultural social facts:
Number of households: (m) 28.8
Average number per household: 2.3
Religion:
Christians: 71.1%

Nonreligious: 21.3%
Muslims: 4.4%
Other: 1.4%
    Hindus: 1.3%
    Jewish: 0.5%
Internet usage: 63,061,419 (2018)
Internet penetration: 94.2 %

The United Kingdom is one of the world's most densely populated countries. Majority of the population live in England. Most of the British are urban-dwelling within London, the nation's capital. As a result of immigration, the UK now has a multiracial society. Immigrants from India, Pakistan, Bangladesh, Sri Lanka, West Indies, and commonwealth countries.

Time is highly valued in UK, with wasted time being considered a wasted resource. Punctuality is an important trait. A firm handshake is the usual greeting for both men and women in professional situations. Maintaining eye contact as you introduce yourself to someone is well-received, but don't stare too much.

Customer experience is critical for business to be successful—particularly mapping customer journeys and content planning.

France

Market facts:
Population: 68,084,217 (2021)
Age structure: <14 = 19%; 15–24 = 12%; 25–54 = 38%; 55–64 = 13%; 65> = 19%
Language: French, Catalonian, Basque, Flemish
Literacy rate: 99.0%

Economic facts:
Principal exports: machinery and transport equipment, chemicals and related products, food, drink and tobacco, mineral fuels and lubricants

Main export destinations: Germany, Belgium, Italy, United
    Kingdom, EU

Principal imports: machinery and transport equipment, min-
    eral fuels and lubricants, chemicals and related products,
    food, drink and tobacco

Main origins of imports: Germany, Belgium, Italy, Netherlands,
    EU

GDP per head: $46,227

Purchasing Power Index:

Economic Freedom Index: 63.8

Structure of employment:
    Service sector: 77.1%
    Industrial sector: 20.3%
    Agricultural sector: 2.6%

Structure of employment rate: (Aged 15–64): 65.9 (2018)

Cultural social facts:

Number of households: (m) 29.3

Average number per household: 2.2

Religion:
    Christians: 63.0%
    Nonreligious: 28.0%
    Muslims: 7.5%
    Other: 1.0%
        Jewish: 0.5%
        Hindus: <0.1%

Internet usage: 60,421,689 (2018)

Internet penetration: 92.3%

The French are of mingled racial type. Distinctive groups
include the Celtic Bretons of Brittany and the Basques living along the
Spanish frontier. The population also includes Algerians, Spaniards,
Italians. Majority of the people live in cities—Paris, Lyons, Marseilles
and Lille. People are increasingly moving from the rural areas into
the cities.

The French are proud of their education system. France is a very hierarchical society. French culture has had worldwide influence on social intercourse, diplomacy, arts, crafts, and architecture since the Middle Ages. The French adhere to a strong and homogeneous set of values. They cherish their culture, history, language, and cuisine, which is considered as an art.

At a business meeting or social meeting, shake hands with everyone present when arriving and leaving. Professionalism is highly valued in business. The French appreciate punctuality. Don't try to mix professional life and private life.

Germany

Market facts:
Population: 83,783,942 (2021)
Age structure: <14 = 13%; 15–24 = 11%; 25–54 = 41%; 55–64
= 14%; 65> = 22%
Language: German, Danish, Frisian, Sorbian, Romany
Literacy rate: 99.0%

Economic facts:
Principal exports: machinery and transport equipment, chemicals and related products, food, drink and tobacco, mineral fuels and lubricants
Main export destinations: France, United Kingdom, Netherlands, United States, EU
Principal imports: machinery and transport equipment, mineral fuels and lubricants, chemicals and related products, food, drink and tobacco
Main origins of imports: Netherlands, France, China, Belgium, EU
GDP per head: $53,694
Purchasing Power Index: 102.36
Economic Freedom Index: 73.5
Structure of employment:
    Service sector: 71.6%

Industrial sector: 27.1%
Agricultural sector: 1.3%
Structure of employment rate: (Aged 15–64): 75.9 (2018)

Cultural social facts:
Number of households: (m) 40.7
Average number per household: 2.0
Religion:
    Christians: 68.7%
    Nonreligious: 24.7%
    Muslims: 5.8%
    Other: 0.5%
        Jewish: 0.3%
        Hindus: <0.1%
Internet usage: 79,127,551
Internet penetration: 96.0%

Majority of the population live in urban areas. Germans are known for their liking of outdoor sports and also for their folk traditions. German culture has made major contributions to European art, thought, science, and especially music, through such composers as Beethoven and Wagner.

An important part of German culture is shaking hands. It is customary to shake someone's hand when you meet them for the first time. Greet your business partners and German coworkers with a firm handshake, a brief nod, and a polite smile, but respect their need for physical distance and personal space. When it comes to meetings, try to be on time as much as possible. Germans are often straightforward and assertive in business setting, but they may not make too much small talk.

German consumers assign to certain issues, mostly privacy. They are concerned about personal data, sustainability.

Ireland

Market facts:
Population: 5,224,844 (2021)
Age structure: <14 = 22%; 15–24 = 12%; 25–54 = 44%; 55–64
   = 10%; 65> = 13%
Language: English, Gaelic
Literacy rate: 99.0%

Economic facts:
Principal exports: chemicals and related products, machinery
   and transport equipment, food, drink and tobacco, raw
   materials
Main export destinations: United States, United Kingdom,
   Belgium, Germany, EU
Principal imports: machinery and transport equipment, chem-
   icals and related products, mineral fuels and lubricants,
   food, drink and tobacco
Main origins of imports: United Kingdom, United States,
   Germany, Netherlands, EU
GDP per head: $55,500
Purchasing Power Index: 80.88
Economic Freedom Index: 80.5
Structure of employment:
   Service sector: 76.5%
   Industrial sector: 18.5%
   Agricultural sector: 5.0%
Structure of employment rate: (Aged 15–64)

Cultural social facts:
Number of households: (m) 1.8
Average number per household: 2.7
Religion:
   Christians: 92.0%,
   Nonreligious: 6.2%
   Muslims: 1.1%

Other: 0.4%
    Hindus: 0.2%
    Jewish: <0.1%
Internet usage: 4,453,436 (2018)
Internet penetration: 91.9%

The Irish is a Celtic people. Majority of the people live in Dublin, Cork, and Limerick. Wherever Irish live, they maintain a vibrant and lively folk culture. The culture of Ireland includes its traditions and customs, as well as folklore, music, language, art, and food.

Irish people quickly speak to each other with the first name. They rarely use terms such as sir or madam. In a meeting, it is customary to shake hands with each person present, both at the beginning and at the end of the meeting.

Italy

Market facts:
Population: 62,390,364 (2021)
Age structure: <14 = 14%; 15–24 = 10%; 25–54 = 43%; 55–64
    = 13%; 65> =21%
Language: Italian, German, French, Slovene
Literacy rate: 99.0%

Economic facts:
Principal exports: machinery and transport equipment, chemicals and related products, food, drink and tobacco, mineral fuels and lubricants
Main export destinations: Germany, France, United States, Switzerland, EU
Principal imports: machinery and transport equipment, mineral fuels and lubricants, chemicals and related products, food, drink and tobacco
Main origins of imports: Germany, France, China, Netherlands, EU

GDP per head: $41,840
Purchasing Power Index: 65.59
Economic Freedom Index: 62.2
Structure of employment:
    Service sector: 70.4%
    Industrial sector: 25.8%
    Agricultural sector: 3.8%
Structure of employment rate: (Aged 15–64 Age): 58.5 (2018)

Cultural social facts:
Number of households: (m) 25.9
Average number per household: 2.3
Religion:
    Christians: 83.3%
    Nonreligious: 12.4%
    Muslims: 3.7%
    Other: 0.4%
        Hindus: 0.1%
        Jewish: <0.1%
Internet usage: 54,798,299 (2018)
Internet penetration: 92.5%

The family is the center of the social culture and provides a stabilizing influence for its members. They are extremely fashion conscious and judge people on their appearance. Upon an introduction and departure, Italian shake hands with everyone individually in a group. Italians will not hesitate to greet people they know with an embrace. One will always be introduced to older people and women first. Do stand when an older person enters the room. Don't ask overly personal questions.

Netherlands

Market facts:
Population: 17,337,340 (2021)

Age structure: <14 = 17%; 15–24 = 12%; 25–54 = 40%; 55–64
= 13%; 65> =18%
Language: Dutch
Literacy rate: 99.0%

Economic facts:
Principal exports: machinery and transport equipment, mineral
fuels and lubricants, chemicals and related products, food,
drink and tobacco
Main export destinations: Germany, Belgium, France, United
Kingdom, EU
Principal imports: machinery and transport equipment, min-
eral fuels and lubricants, chemicals and related products,
food, drink and tobacco
Main origins of imports: Germany, China, Belgium, United
Kingdom, EU GDP per head: $59,299
Purchasing Power Index: 90.73
Economic Freedom Index: 76.8
Structure of employment:
Service sector: 81.4%
Industrial sector: 16.6%
Agricultural sector: 2.2%
Structure of employment rate: (Aged 15–64): 77.5 (2018)

Cultural social facts:
Number of households: (m) 7.8
Average number per household: 2.2
Religion:
Christians: 50.6%,
Nonreligious: 42.1%
Muslims: 6.0%
Other: 0.6%
Hindus: 0.5%
Jewish: 0.2%
Internet usage: 16,383,879 (2019)
Internet penetration: 95.6%

Nearly half the population live close to the three larger cities—Amsterdam, The Hague, and Rotterdam. People are modest, tolerant, independent, self-reliant, and entrepreneurial. They value education, hard work, ambition, and ability. They expect eye contact while speaking with someone. The Dutch take punctuality for business meetings very seriously and expect that you will do likewise. The Dutch are conservative and forceful and can be stubborn and tough negotiators.

They shake hands with everyone present at business meetings. They shake hands again when leaving. Dutch people are reserved and don't touch in public or display anger or extreme exuberance.

Japan

Market facts:
Population: 126,476,461 (2021)
Age structure: <14 = 13%; 15–24 = 10%; 25–54 = 38%; 55–64 = 13%; 65> = 27%
Language: Japanese
Literacy rate: 99.0%

Economic facts:
Principal exports: capital equipment, industrial supplies, consumer durable goods, consumer nondurable goods
Main export destinations: China, United States, South Korea, Thailand, Hong Kong
Principal imports: industrial supplies, capital equipment, food and direct consumer goods, consumer durable goods
Main origins of imports: China, United States, Australia, Saudi Arabia, United Arab Emirates
GDP per head: $42,197
Purchasing Power Index: 87.28
Economic Freedom Index: 72.1(2019)
Structure of employment:
    Service sector: 72.1%
    Industrial sector: 24.5%

Agricultural sector: 3.4%
Structure of employment rate: (Aged 15–64): 76.8 (2018)

Cultural social facts:
Number of households: (m) 53.4
Average number per household: 2.4
Religion:
    Nonreligious: 57.0%
    Buddhists: 36.2%
    Other: 5.0%
        Christians: 1.6%
        Muslims: 0.2%
        Jewish: <0.1%
Internet usage: 118,626,672 (2018)
Internet penetration: 93.5%

The Japanese are basically a Mongoloid race. Most Japanese live in Tokyo, Osaka, and Yokohama. Japanese culture is characterized by moderate power distance, moderate individualism, very high masculinity, very high uncertainty avoidance, and a high long-term orientation. Japanese companies tend to be hierarchical, and showing respect to senior executives is a key part of building a good business relationship.

Japan is a relationship-based business culture. Japanese value their relationships with coworkers, partners, and bosses over any given goals. Japanese usually request for introduction/referrals from someone they know rather than go online. They are interested in smart sensors, connected instruments, and factory automation. In Japan, decision-making is much smaller than US. Decision-making processes are like consensus building and "bottom up" take time.

Japanese executives put much more faith in information they get directly from wholesales and retailers in the distribution channels. They track what's happening among channels' members on a monthly, weekly, and sometimes even daily basis. Japanese-style of market research relies heavily on two kinds of information: *soft data*, obtained from visits to dealers and other channels' members; *hard data* is about shipments, inventory levels, and retail sales/marketing data. Japanese management believe that their data better reflects the behavior and intention of consumers.

Avoid losing your temper. Japanese partners may interpret this as a sign of weakness, or worse, an insult. Long silence is common during negotiations in Japan, where building a consensus among staff before taking a decision is valid.

South Korea

Market facts:
Population: 51,715,162 (2021)
Age structure: <14 = 14%; 15–24 = 14%; 25–54 = 47%; 55–64 = 13%; 65> = 13%
Language: Korean, English
Literacy rate:

Economic facts:
Principal exports: machinery and transport equipment, manufactured goods, chemicals and related products, mineral fuels and lubricants
Main export destinations: China, United States, Japan, Hong Kong
Principal imports: mineral fuels and lubricants, Machinery & transport equip., Manufactured-goods, Chemicals & related products
Main origins of imports: China, Japan, United States, Saudi Arabia
GDP per head: $43,124
Purchasing Power Index: 85.21 Economic Freedom Index: 72.3 (2019)
Structure of employment:
    Service sector: 70.1%
    Industrial sector: 24.9%
    Agricultural sector: 4.9%
Structure of employment rate: (Aged 15–64): 66.6 (2018)

Cultural social facts:
Number of households: (m) 20.5
Average number per household: 2.5
Religion:
    Nonreligious: 46.4%
    Christians: 29.4%
    Buddhists: 22.9%
    Other: 1.0%
        Muslims: 0.2%
        Jewish: <0.1%
Internet usage: 49,234,329 (2019)
Internet penetration: 95.9%

Family is the most important part of Korean society, and the father is the leader of the family. They also believe in a hierarchical structure, and children help their parents and must obey them and show respect to the elders. They believe in sincerity and loyalty and follow certain codes of conduct while meeting, eating, praying and even celebrating. At times when many other cultures would shake hands, Koreans bow. They bow as a sign of gratitude and respect to the person they are meeting. Allow other people to introduce you when meeting new people and clients.

India

Market facts:
Population: 1,380,004,385 (2021)
Age structure: <14 = 28%; 15–24 = 18%; 25–54 = 41%; 55–64
    = 7%; 65> = 6%
Language: Hindi, Bengali, Telugu, Marathi, Tamil, Urdu,
    Gujarati
English Literacy rate: 72.2%

Economic facts:
Principal exports: engineering products, petroleum and prod-
    ucts, gems and jewelry, agricultural products

Main export destinations: United Arab Emirates, United States, China, Singapore

Principal imports: petroleum and products, gold and silver, electronic goods, machinery

Main origins of imports: China, United Arab Emirates, Saudi Arabia, Switzerland

GDP per head: $6,454

Purchasing Power Index: 54.30

Economic Freedom Index: 55.2 (2019)

Structure of employment:

Service sector: 31.5%

Industrial sector: 24.7%

Agricultural sector: 43.9%

Structure of employment rate: (Aged 15–64): 46.3 (2018)

Cultural social facts:

Number of households: 278.2 (m)

Average number per household: 4.8

Religion:

Hindus: 79.5%,

Muslims: 14.4%,

Others: 3.6%,

Christians: 2.5%,

Jewish: <0.1%,

Nonreligious: <0.1%

Internet usage: 560,000,000 (2019)

Internet penetration: 40.9%

Majority of the people live in villages. Indian has twenty-nine states with different cultures. The Indian culture is often labelled as an amalgamation of several various cultures. India is a hierarchical society. Societal hierarchy is evident in caste groups, among individuals, and in family and kinship groups.

Indian society attaches a lot of value to status, so people in positions of power often have more room to play than the average citizen. Be reserved when shaking hands with those of the opposite gender.

You are better to wait until your host or hostess extends their hand to you. Preferably, reserve your business meetings one or two months ahead.

Pakistan

Market facts:

Population: 238,181,034 (2021)

Age structure: <14 = 33%; 15–24 = 22%; 25–54 = 36%; 55–64 = 5%; 65> = 4%

Language: Punjabi, Sindhi, Saraiki, Pashtu, Urdu, Balochi, Hindko

English Literacy rate: 56.4%

Economic facts:

Principal exports: cotton fabrics, knitwear, cotton yarn and thread, rice

Main export destinations: United States, China, United Arab Emirates, Afghanistan

Principal imports: petroleum products, crude oil, palm oil, telecoms equipment

Main origins of imports: China, Saudi Arabia, United Arab Emirates, Kuwait

GDP per head: $1,482

Purchasing Power Index: 30.57

Economic Freedom Index: 55.0

Structure of employment:

　　Service sector: 34.7%

　　Industrial sector: 23.6%

　　Agricultural sector: 41.7%

Structure of employment rate: (Aged 15–64):

Cultural social facts:

Number of households: 29.4 (m)

Average number of households: 6.7

Religion:
  Muslims: 96.4%
  Hindus: 1.9%
  Christians: 1.6%
  Jewish: <0.1%
  Nonreligious: <0.1%
  Others: <0.1%
Internet usage: 71,608,065 (2019)
Internet penetration: 32.4%

In Pakistan, social organization revolves around kinship rather than around the caste system in India. Most people live with large extended families.

Men shake hands with each other and often hug when a relationship is formed. Men should not attempt to shake a woman's hand unless she extends hers first. In Pakistani business culture, people are rarely addressed by their first names. Instead, refer to an associate by their title and surname. Trust is important in the Pakistanis' business world.

Avid controversial topics such as politics, religion, or terrorism. Business meetings are best planned for the late morning or early afternoons. Don't feel uncomfortable if colleagues stand very close as this is common.

Singapore

Market facts:
Population: 5,866,139 (2021)
Age structure: < 14 = 13%; 15–24 = 18%; 25–54 = 50%; 55–64
  = 10%; 65 > = 9%
Language: Mandarin, English, Malay, Tamil, Hokkien, Cantonese
Literacy rate: 96.8%

Economic facts:
Principal exports: mineral fuels, electronic components and parts, chemicals and products, manufactured products

Main export destinations: Malaysia, China, Hong Kong, Indonesia, United States

Principal imports: machinery and transport equipment, mineral fuels, miscellaneous manufactured articles, manufactured products

Main origins of imports: Malaysia, China, United State, South Korea, Japan

GDP per head: $98,526

Purchasing Power Index: 88.96

Economic Freedom Index: 89.4 (2019)

Structure of employment:
  Service sector: 82.9%
  Industrial sector: 16.6%
  Agricultural sector: 0.5%

Structure of employment rate (Aged 15–64):

Cultural social facts:

Number of households: 1.3 (m)

Average number per household: 4.4

Religion:
  Buddhists: 33.9%
  Christians: 18.2%
  Nonreligious: 16.4%
  Muslims: 14.3%
  Others: 12.0%
     Hindus: 5.2%

Internet usage: 5,173,907 (2019)

Internet penetration: 88.4%

Singapore is a secular immigrant country. The culture of Singapore is a combination of Asian and European cultures. Influenced by Malay, South Asian, East Asian, and Eurasian cultures.

When you organize a business meeting with a prospective client or business partner, you should make sure to schedule your appointments at least two weeks ahead. Always try to be punctual, or even a little bit early. It is important to respect the hierarchy within a company you are doing business with. Never raise your voice, get aggressive, or push your business partner to reach a decision. In Singapore, business is done at a rather slow pace, and you should try to be patient.

Malaysia

Market facts:
Population: 33,519,426 (2021)
Age structure: <14 = 29%; 15–24 = 17%; 25–54 = 41%; 55–64 = 8%; 65> = 6%
Language: Bahasa Malaysia, English, Chinese, Tamils, Telugu
Literacy rate: 94.6%

Economic facts:
Principal exports: machinery and transport equipment, mineral fuels, manufactured goods, chemicals
Main export destinations: Singapore, China, Japan, United States
Principal imports: machinery and transport equipment, mineral fuels, manufactured goods, chemicals
Main origins of imports: China, Singapore, Japan, United States
GDP per head: $27,887
Purchasing Power Index: 65.32
Economic Freedom Index: 74.0
Structure of employment:
    Service sector: 61.6%
    Industrial sector: 27.3%
    Agricultural sector: 11.1%
Structure of employment rate (Aged 15–64):

Cultural social facts:
Number of households: 7.7 (m)
Average number per household: 4.1
Religion:
    Muslims: 63.7%

Buddhists: 17.7%
Christians: 9.4%
Hindus: 6.0%
Others: 2.5%
    Nonreligious: 0.7%
Internet usage: 26,353,017 (2019)
Internet penetration: 81.4%

Malaysia is a multicultural nation. Greeting in a social contact will depend upon the ethnicity of the person that one is meeting. In general, most Malays are aware of Western ways, so the handshake is normal. Malay woman may not shake hands with men due to their cultural belief. Handshakes are generally accepted for both men and women. While business culture remains hierarchical, teamwork and collaboration are encouraged with all members of the organization being valued. Business etiquette is marked by sensitivity and diplomacy.

Business meetings usually convene on time. Do remain polite and respectful in all situations. Don't be impatient and aggressive.

Indonesia

Market facts:
Population: 275,122,131 (2021)
Age structure: <14 = 26%; 15–24 = 17%; 25–54 = 42%; 55–64
    = 8%; 65> = 7%
Language: Bahasa Indonesia, English, Dutch
Literacy rate: 95.4%

Economic facts:
Principal exports: mineral fuels, machinery and transport equipment, manufactured goods, animal and vegetable oils
Main export destinations: Japan, China, Singapore, United States
Principal imports: machinery and transport equipment, mineral fuels, manufactured goods, chemicals and related products

Main origins of imports: China, Singapore, Japan, Malaysia
GDP per head: $12,073
Purchasing Power Index: 25.5
Economic Freedom Index: 64.8 (2019)
Structure of employment:
Service sector: 47.5%
Industrial sector: 22.0%
Agricultural sector: 30.5%
Structure of employment rate: (Aged 15–64 Age)

Cultural social facts:
Number of households: 66.9 (m)
Average number per household: 3.9
Religion:
Muslims: 87.2%
Christians: 9.9%
Hindus: 1.7%
Others: 1.1%
Jewish: <0.1%
Nonreligious: <0.1%
Internet usage: 171,260,000 (2019)
Internet penetration: 63.5%

Two-thirds of the population live on Java, the site of the capital and chief port Jakarta. The population can be broadly divided into Malays and Papuans with Chinese, Arabs, and others.

The culture of Indonesia has been shaped by long interaction between original indigenous customs and multiple foreign influences. Indonesian people are friendly. Handshakes are usually an adequate way of introduction. People appreciate polite smiles of foreigners they are introducing, and they will certainly give you a smile back.

Australia

Market facts:
Population: 25,088,636 (2021)

Age structure: <14 = 18%; 15–24 = 13%; 25–54 = 42%; 55–64
    = 12%; 65> = 16%
Language: English, Chinese, Italian, Arabic, Greek, Vietnamese
Literacy rate: 99.0%

Economic facts:
Principal exports: crude materials, fuels, food, manufactured
    goods
Main export destinations: China, Japan, South Korea, India
Principal imports: machinery and transport equipment, mineral
    fuels, Miscellaneous manufactured articles, Manufactured
    goods
Main origins of imports: China, United States, Japan, Singapore
GDP per head: $65,400
Purchasing Power Index:
Economic Freedom Index: 80.4 (2019)
Structure of employment:
    Service sector: 78.1%
    Industrial sector: 19.4%
    Agricultural sector: 2.6%
Structure of employment rate (Aged 15–64): 73.8 (2018)

Cultural social facts:
Number of households: 9.9 (m)
Average number per household: 2.5
Religion:
    Christians: 67.3%
    Nonreligious: 24.2%
    Others: 4.2%
        Muslims: 2.4%
        Hindus: 1.4%
        Jewish: 0.5%
Internet usage: 21,711,706 (2018)
Internet penetration: 87.8%

The people are mainly of British origins, but there are aborigines and many immigrants from Italy, Greece, Germany, Netherlands, and the US. Most of the population is concentrated in the coastal cities—Sydney, Brisbane. Australia is a multicultural society. Australians tend to be fairly informal in their everyday interactions, and it's common practice to call someone by their first name only.

Greetings are casual and relaxed in handshakes, and a smile is appropriate. Australians are very straightforward when it comes to business. They are receptive to new ideas. Try to be factual, friendly, and to the point, avoiding self-importance. The decision-making will be slower than usual, as the work environment in Australia business culture is collaborative.

Don't try to rush the decision-making—patience is very much appreciated.

New Zealand

Market facts:
Population: 4,991,442 (2021)
Age structure: < 14 = 20%; 15–24 = 14%; 25–54 = 40%; 55–64 = 12%; 65> = 15%
Language: English, Mauri, Asian, Pacific
Literacy rate: 99.0%

Economic facts:
Principal exports: dairy products, meat, forestry products, wool
Main export destinations: Australia, China, United States, Japan
Principal imports: machinery and electrical equipment, mineral fuels, transport equipment
Main origins of imports: China, Australia, United States, Japan
GDP per head: $44,252
Purchasing Power Index: 92.66
Economic Freedom Index: 84.4 (2019)
Structure of employment:
Service sector: 73.4%
Industrial sector: 20.4%

Agricultural sector: 6.2%
Structure of employment rate (Aged 15–64): 77.5 (2018)

Cultural social facts:
Number of households: 1.7 (m)
Average number per household: 2.8
Religion:
    Christian: 57.0%
    Nonreligious: 36.6%
    Others: 2.8%
        Hindus: 2.1%
        Muslims: 1.2%
        Jewish: 0.2%
Internet usage: 4,351,987 (2018)
Internet penetration: 90.8%

About 16 percent to 20 percent of the New Zealand's population are Maoris, and the remaining are descended from settlers who came from Britain. Majority of the people live in Auckland, Christchurch, and Wellington. New Zealanders are friendly and outgoing.

Greetings are usually casual and consist of a handshake and direct eye contact. Women are treated as equals in the workplace, often rising to senior corporate positions. The business culture conforms to typically British models. The general approach to management in New Zealand is hierarchical, with decisions being made by senior-level executives.

Egypt

Market facts:
Population: 106,437,241 (2021)
Age structure: < 14 = 32%; 15–24 = 18%; 25–54 = 39$; 55–64
    = 7%; 65> = 5%
Language: Arabic, English, French
Literacy rate: 75.8%

Economic facts:

Principal exports: petroleum and products, finished goods including textiles, semi-finished products, iron and steel

Main export destinations: Italy, India, United States, Saudi Arabia

Principal imports: intermediate goods, consumer goods, fuels, capital goods

Main origins of imports: China, United States, Ukraine, Turkey

GDP per head: $2,549

Purchasing Power Index: 22.51

Economic Freedom Index: 52.5 (2019)

Structure of employment:

    Service sector: 48.6%

    Industrial sector: 26.6%

    Agricultural sector: 24.9%

Structure of employment rate (Aged 15–64):

Cultural facts:

Number of households: 23.5 (m) Average number per household: 4.2

Religion:

    Muslims: 94.9%

    Christians: 5.1%

    Hindus: <0.1%

    Jewish: <0.1%

    Nonreligious: <0.1%

    Others: <0.1%

Internet usage: 49,231,493

Internet penetration: 48.1%

People are mainly of Hamitic origins. There are Greek, Armenians, and others living in Egypt. They are generally very helpful and polite. When it comes to family affairs, family is very important, so they pay special attention to family values and relationships.

Since there are plenty of greeting styles in Egypt, it is safest to wait for your counterpart to initiate the greeting, especially at a first meeting. Try to avoid inquiring about the female members of their family. Punctuality is not considered the main priority. Do make eye contact when meeting with your business associates, especially with male colleagues.

Israel

Market facts:
Population: 8,787,045 (2021)
Age structure: <14 = 28%; 15–24 = 16%; 25–54 = 37%; 55–64 = 9%; 65> = 11%
Language: Hebrew, Arabic, English
Literacy rate: 97.8%

Economic facts:
Principal exports: chemicals and chemical products, polished diamonds, communications, medical and scientific equipment, electronics
Main export destinations: United States, Hong Kong, United Kingdom, Belgium
Principal imports: fuel, diamonds, machinery and equipment, chemicals
Main origins of imports: United States, China, Germany, Switzerland
GDP per head: $41,855
Purchasing Power Index: 78.09
Economic Freedom Index: 72.8 (2019)
Structure of employment:
   Service sector: 81.7%
   Industrial sector: 17.3%
   Agricultural sector: 1.0%
Structure of employment rate: (Aged 15–64): 69.0 (2018)

Cultural social facts:
Number of households: 2.5 (m)
Average number per household: 3.3

Religion: Jewish: 75.6%
  Muslims: 18.6%
  Nonreligious: 3.1%
  Christians: 2.0%
  Others: 0.6%
    Hindus: <0.1%
Internet usage: 6,740,287 (2018)
Internet penetration: 78.5%

Majority of the people were born in Israel. The remainder are immigrants, mostly from Central and Eastern Europe, the Middle East, North Africa, and Russia. Minorities include Christians, Muslim Arabs, Druze, Circassians, and Samaritans. Most of the population is urban, living mostly in Tel Aviv, Jaffa, Haifa, and Jerusalem. Jews in rural areas generally live in Kibbutzim and Moshavim.

Israelis welcome to use the Israeli greeting, "Shalom." It will help you blend with locals. Shaking hands is the normal way of greeting. Israeli businesses are motivated and ambitious. Since many Israelis will respond more to a relationship-oriented meeting, you should treat your Israeli business partners more like friends than clients. The atmosphere of Israeli businesses and business meeting is fairly relaxed. In general, Israelis are direct and state their opinions. You should try to do the same. Israelis will trust you more if you are honest and direct.

Brazil

Market facts:
Population: 212,559,417 (2021)
Age structure: < 14 = 23%; 15–24 = 17%; 25–54 = 44%; 55–64 = 9%; 65 >= 8%
Language: Portuguese
Literacy rate: 92.6%

Economic facts:
Principal exports: primary products, manufactured products, semi-manufactured products

Main export destinations: China, United States, Argentina, Netherlands

Principal imports: intermediate products and raw materials, capital goods, consumer goods, fuels and lubricants

Main origins of imports: China, United States, Argentina, Germany

GDP per head: $15,600

Purchasing Power Index: 32.81

Economic Freedom Index: 51.9 (2019)

Structure of employment:

Service sector: 70.2%

Industrial sector: 20.4%

Agricultural sector: 9.4%

Structure of employment rate: (Aged 15–64): 61.6 (2018)

Cultural social facts:

Number of households: 62.1 (m)

Average number per household: 3.3

Religion:

Christians: 88.9%,

Nonreligious: 7.9%

Others: 3.1%

Hindus: <0.1%

Jewish: <0.1%

Muslims: <0.1%

Internet usage: 149,057,635 (2018)

Internet penetration: 70.1%

Brazil is different from its Spanish-speaking neighbors in having a racially integrated population. This consists of a three-fold mixture: Portuguese intermarried both with the native Indians and with the black slaves imported from West Africa.

The culture of the Indigenous Indians, Africans, and Portuguese have together formed the modern Brazilian way of life. Brazilians continue to be exuberant and creative in their cultures and art forms. The family structure and values are important. They tend to be affectionate, tactile people with a smaller sense of personal space. There is a level of informality in how they greet and address each other. Shaking hands, hugs, and kisses on cheeks are common greetings though women tend to touch more and greet with kisses.

Demonstrate strong character and enjoyable personality. Develop a personal relationship before getting to business. Don't discuss about personal lives. Avoid confronting a Brazilian negotiator.

Chile

Market facts:
Population: 19,116,201 (2021)
Age structure: < 14 = 21%; 15–24 = 16%; 25–54 = 43%; 55–64 = 10%; 65 > = 10%
Language: Spanish, English, Indigenous
Literacy rate: 96.6%

Economic facts:
Principal exports: copper, fresh fruit, paper products
Main export destinations: China, United States, Japan, South Korea, Brazil
Principal imports: intermediate goods, consumer goods, capital goods
Main origins of imports: United States, China, Argentina, Brazil, Germany
GDP per head: $25,068
Purchasing Power Index: 42.50
Economic Freedom Index: 75.4
Structure of employment:
    Service sector: 68.1%
    Industrial sector: 22.7%
    Agricultural sector: 9.2%
Structure of employment rate (Aged 15–64): 62.6 (2018)

Cultural social facts:
Number of households: 6.4 (m)

Average number per household: 2.8
Religion:
    Christians: 89.4%
    Nonreligious: 8.6%
    Others: 1.9%
        Jewish: 0.1%
        Hindus: <0.1%
        Muslims: <0.1%
Internet usage: 17,671,546 (2019)
Internet penetration: 92.4%

Majority of the people live in Santiago, Valparaiso. Seventy percent of the population is mixed Spanish Indian blood, and other thirty percent being mainly of Spanish or other European origin. Chilean culture has been a mix of Spanish colonial elements with indigenous Mapuchi culture, as well as that of other immigrant cultures.

Make direct eye contact while having a conversation with business associates you meet. Do be on time for business meetings. Don't talk about politics or human rights. Do always greet the most senior person first.

Peru

Market facts:
Population: 32,933,835 (2021)
Age structure: < 14 = 27%; 15–24 = 19%; 25–54 = 40%; 55–64
    = 8%; 65 > = 7%
Language: Spanish, Quechua, Aymasa
Literacy rate: 94.4%

Economic facts:
Principal exports: copper, gold, fishmeal, zinc
Main export destinations: China, United States, Canada, Japan
Principal imports: intermediate goods, capital goods, consumer
    goods, other goods

Main origins of imports: United States, China, Brazil, Argentina
GDP per head: $12,200
Purchasing Power Index: 33.95
Economic Freedom Index: 67.8
Structure of employment:
    Service sector: 56.9%
    Industrial sector: 15.6%
    Agricultural sector: 22.5%
Structure of employment rate (Aged 15–64):

Cultural social facts:
Number of households: 8.4 (m)
Average number per household: 3.8
Religion:
Christians- 95.5%
Nonreligious- 8.0%
Others: 1.5%
Hindus: <0.1%
Jewish: <0.1%
Muslims: <0.1%
Internet usage: 22,000,000 (2018)
Internet penetration: 66.8%

Peru's population is composed of about fifty percent Amerindians, forty percent Mestizos (mixed white and Indians), and ten percent white. Peru is a very conservative and religious country. As in most South American countries, a single kiss on the left cheek is the standard greeting between woman and man, and between two men, a handshake is the go-to approach.

Peruvians belong to hierarchical culture when authority is expected to be respected. In formal business meeting settings, it's best to wait until someone invites you to use first names. Be tactful and diplomatic in business dealings.

South Africa

Market facts:
Population: 59,308,690 (2021)
Age structure: < 14 = 29%; 15–24 = 19%; 25–54 = 41%; 55–64
    = 7%; 65 > = 6%
Language: Isi Zulu, Isi Xhosa, English, Afrikaans
Literacy rate: 94.6%

Economic facts:
Principal exports: gold, coal, platinum, car and other components
Main export destinations: China, United States, Japan, India
Principal imports: petrochemicals, petroleum oils and other, car
    and other components, equipment components for cars
Main origins of imports: China, Germany, Saudi Arabia, United
    States
GDP per head: $6,374
Purchasing Power Index: 73.61
Economic Freedom Index: 58.3
Structure of employment:
    Service sector: 71.6%
    Industrial sector: 23.2%
    Agricultural sector: 5.2%
Structure of employment rate (Aged 15–64): 43.2 (2018)

Cultural social facts:
Number of households: 16.9 (m)
Average number per household: 3.4
Religion:
    Christians: 81.2%
    Nonreligious: 14.9%
    Muslims: 1.7%
    Hindus: 1.1%
    Other: 0.9%
        Jewish: 0.1%

Internet usage: 32,615,165 (2018)
Internet penetration: 35.9%

Majority of South Africans are Zulu and Xhosa. Others include white, mixed descent, and Asiatic. The culture of South Africa is known for its ethnic and cultural diversity. South Africans have become increasingly urbanized and westernized; aspects of traditional culture have declined.

South Africans are very friendly and may express affection openly. It is important to always show respect to elders, even if they are not part of the company. Never raise your voice and always keep a mild tone when conversing.

Argentina

Market facts:
Population: 45,864,941 (2021)
Age structure: <14 = 25%; 15–24 = 16%; 25–54 = 39%; 55–64 = 9%; 65 > = 12%
Language: Spanish, English, German, French, Indigenous
Literacy rate: 98.1%

Economic facts:
Principal exports: processed agricultural products, manufactures, primary products, fuels
Main export destinations: Brazil, China, Chile, United States
Principal imports: intermediate goods, capital goods, fuels, consumer goods
Main origins of imports: Brazil, China, United States, Germany
GDP per head: $22,600
Purchasing Power Index: 47.2
Economic Freedom Index: 52.2 (2019)
Structure of employment:
  Service sector: 77.5%
  Industrial sector: 22.4%
  Agricultural sector: 0.1%

Structure of employment rate (Aged 15–64):

Cultural social facts:
Number of households: 13.8 (m)
Average number per household: 3.2
Religion:
    Christians: 85.2%
    Nonreligious: 12.2%
    Other: 1.1%
        Muslims: 1.0%
        Jewish: 0.5%
        Hindus: <0.1%
Internet usage:
Internet penetration: 92.0%

About 90 percent of the people are descended from south European immigrants. There are native Indians living in Argentina. Majority of people live in urban areas. Argentina's culture has been strongly influenced by its mostly European immigrant people, although it most certainly emerges from its Latin roots with a strong South Americans flair.

The people emphasize the individual's role in society and view the individual who is independent as capable. Family is central to the live of average citizen. Do expect a one kiss on the cheek for greeting since it's the typical and normal greeting. Don't be offended by Argentines' open, direct, and loud communication style. Don't be intimidated when Argentines look you directly in the eye in public places. Don't voice your opinion on Argentines' politics or religions.

COUNTRIES OF MONOCRATIC SYSTEM

China

Market facts:
Population: 1,439,323,776 (2021)
Age structure: <14 = 17%; 15–24 = 14%; 25–54 = 48%, 55–64
    = 11%; 65 > = 10%
Language: Mandarin, Cantonese, Minbei, Minnan
Literacy rate: 96.4%

Economic facts:
Principal exports: electrical goods, telecoms equipment, office
    machinery, clothing and apparel,
Main export destinations: United States, Hong Kong, Japan,
    South Korea, EU
Principal imports: electrical machinery, petroleum and prod-
    ucts, metal ores and scrap, professional instruments
Main origins of imports: Japan, South Korea, Taiwan, United
    States, EU
GDP per head: $17,312
Purchasing power Index: 60.88
Economic Freedom Index: 58.4 (2019)
Structure of employment:
    Service sector: 44.6%
    Industrial sector: 28.6%
    Agricultural sector: 26.8%
Structure of employment rate: (Aged 15–64): 75.1 (2018)

Cultural social facts:
Number of households: 466.8 (m)
Average number per household: 3.0

Religion:
   Nonreligious: 52.2%
   Other: 22.7%
      Buddhists: 18.2%
      Christians: 5.1%
      Muslims: 1.8%
      Jewish: <0.1%
Internet usage: 854,000,000 (2019)
Internet penetration: 59.3%

The China belongs to the Mongoloid race. There are sizeable minorities of Mongols and Tibetans. Social customs in China: Chinese consider it rude to look someone directly into the eyes, cross your arms or legs, or have your hands in pocket when you are speaking to someone. The Chinese put a tremendous emphasis on family ties.

They shake hands upon meetings. They may nod or bow instead of shaking hands. Do address the Chinese by their professional titles and last name. Don't be late. Meetings always begin on time. Punctuality is important. Being late is considered rude. Don't interrupt any period of silence at a business meeting. Don't expect easy negotiations.

Chinese customers understand brands. Chinese culture places great emphasis on symbolism and symbolic values. Buying power has increased by an order of magnitude. They are smart and well-educated and have a broad knowledge of the outside world. They use online/digital marketing; WeChat is the biggest social media platform. Large search engines are Baidu and Qihoo; Sina Weibo is the local hybrid of Facebook; Youku is the Chinese YouTube. Seventy percent or more of the e-commerce market share is held by Alibaba which sells more products from its Taobao and Tmall platforms. Payment system via online include Ali Pay and WeChat pay; Ten Cent is the maker of WeChat.

Russia

Market facts:
Population: 143,895,551 (2021)
Age structure: <14 = 17%; 15–24 = 10%; 25–54 = 46%, 55–64
    = 9%; 65 > = 14%
Language: Russian, Tatar
Literacy rate: 99.7%

Economic facts:
Principal exports: fuels, manufactures, ores and metals, food,
    agricultural raw materials
Main export destinations: Netherlands, China, Italy, Germany
Principal imports: manufactures, food, ores and metals, agricul-
    tural raw materials, fuels
Main origins of imports: Chin, Germany, Ukraine, Italy
GDP per head: $28,213
Purchasing Power Index: 38.94
Economic Freedom Index: 58.9 (2019)
Structure of employment:
    Service sector: 67.2%
    Industrial sector: 26.9%
    Agricultural sector: 5.8%
Structure of employment rate (Aged 15–64): 71.0 (2018)

Cultural social facts:
Number of households: 57.2 (m)
Average number per household: 2.5
Religion:
Christians: 73.3%
Nonreligious: 16.2%
Muslims: 10.0%
Jewish: 0.2%
Hindus: <0.1%
Other: <0.1%

Internet usage: 109,552,842 (2018)
Internet penetration: 6.1%

The typical greeting is a firm, almost bone-crushing handshake while maintaining direct eye contact and giving the appropriate greeting for the time of the day. When men shake hands with women, the handshake is less firm.

It is different to do business without the help from a local connection. Patience is important with Russians; negotiations can often be slow. Avoid hard selling techniques and any sort of conflict or confrontation.

Russians don't usually make an immediate decision in a meeting; usually, a certain amount of deliberation is done in private afterward.

Avoid topics such as your complaints about Russia, the Holocaust, Czars and monarchy, conflicts with ethnic minorities, and comparing Russia to other developing countries.

DPRK/North Korea

Market facts:
Population: 25,831,360 (2021)
Age structure: < 14 = 21%; 15–24 = 16%; 25–54 = 44%; 55–64
    = 9%; 65 > = 10%
Language: Korean
Literacy rate: 100.0%

Economic facts:
Principal exports:
Main export destinations:
Principal imports:
Main origins of imports:
GDP per head: $1,800
Purchasing Power Index:
Economic Freedom Index: 5.9 (2019)
Structure of employment rate (Aged 15–64)

Cultural social facts:
Internet usage: 20,000 (2019)
Internet penetration: 0.1%

North Korea (DPRK) has received a continuous stream of foreign cultural influence mainly from China. Koreans have kept their identity and maintained and developed their unique language and customs.

Vietnam

Market facts:
Population: 102,789,598 (2021)
Age structure: < 14 = 24%; 15–24 = 17%; 25–54 = 45%; 55–64 = 8%; 65 > = 6%
Language: Vietnamese, English, French, Chinese, Khmer
Literacy rate: 95.4%

Economic facts:
Principal exports: textiles and garments, crude oil, footwear, fisheries products
Main export destinations: United States, Japan, China, South Korea, Germany
Principal imports: machinery and equipment, petroleum products, textiles, steel
Main origins of imports: China, South Korea, Japan, Singapore, Thailand
GDP per head: $2,566
Purchasing Power Index: 2814
Economic Freedom Index: 55.3 (2019)
Structure of employment:
    Service sector: 34.4%
    Industrial sector: 25.8%
    Agricultural sector: 39.8%
Structure of employment rate: (Aged 15–64)

Cultural social facts:
Number of households: 28.9 (m)
Average number per household: 3.3
Religion:
    Other: 45.6%
        Buddhists: 16.4%
        Non-religion: 29.6%
        Christians: 8.2%
        Muslims: 0.2%
        Jewish: <0.1%
Internet usage: 68,541,344 (2018)
Internet penetration: 70.4%

The oldest male in the family is the head of the family and the most important family member. Respect for parents and ancestors is a key virtue in Vietnam. Appointments are required and should be made several weeks ahead. They are punctual and expect others to be. Handshakes are used upon meeting and departing. Relationships are critical to successful business partnerships. Negotiations can be slow.

Cuba

Market facts:
Population: 11,492,046 (2021)
Age structure: < 14 = 16%; 15–24 = 14%; 25–54 = 47%; 55–64 = 11%; 65 >= 13%
Language: Spanish
Literacy rate: 99.7%

Economic facts:
Principal exports:
Main export destinations:
Principal imports:
Main origins of imports:
GDP per head: N/A
Purchasing Power Index:

Economic Freedom Index: 27.8 (2019)
Structure of employment rate: (Aged 15–64)

Cultural social facts:
Religion: Roman Catholics
Internet usage: 5,642,595 (2018)
Internet penetration: 49.1%

Cuba is well-known for its vibrant and rich culture that is a complex mixture of different influences and factors. The unique and vibrant culture is influenced heavily by Latin Americans, Europeans, Africans, and in Indigenous American cultures.

Venezuela

Market facts:
Population: 29,069,153 (2021)
Age structure: < 14 = 28%; 15–24 = 19%; 25–54 = 40%; 55–64 = 8%; 65 > = 6%
Language: Spanish, Indigenous
Literacy rate: 95.4%

Economic facts:
Principal exports: oil, non-oil
Main export destinations: United States, China, India, Netherlands Antilles
Principal imports: intermediate goods, capital goods, consumer goods
Main origins of imports: United States, China, Brazil, Colombia
GDP per head: N/A
Purchasing Power Index:
Economic Freedom Index: 25.9 (2019)
Structure of employment:
    Service sector: 71.7%
    Industrial sector: 21.1%
    Agricultural sector: 7.2%

Structure of employment rate: (Aged 15–64)

Cultural social facts:
Number of households: 8.6 (m)
Average number per household: 3.7
Religion: Christians: 89.3%
Nonreligious: 10.0%
Muslims: 0.3%
Hindus: <0.1%
Jewish: <0.1%
Internet usage: 23,601,504 (2019)
Internet penetration: 83.0%

The population is mainly Mestizos. The country has a diverse and complex culture that is influenced by the cultures of large number of ethnic groups living in the country. They are outgoing and friendly nature. They are known to stand in close proximity and to use hand gestures, even touching, when in conversation. Men greet each other with a firm handshake, and in some cases, a hug depending on the status of the person. The country has a strong defined socioeconomic class structure that is often divided along gender and ethnicity. Shake hands when meeting someone for the first time. Keep eye contact.

Syria

Market facts:
Population: 21,384,316 (2021)
Age structure: < 14 = 33%, 15–24 = 20%; 25–54 = 39%; 55–64 = 5%; 65 > = 4%
Language: Arabic, Kurdish, Armenian, Aramaic, Circassian, French, English
Literacy rate: 86.3%

Economic facts:
Principal exports:
Main export destinations:
Principal imports:
Main origins of imports:
GDP per head: $5,100
Purchasing Power Index:
Economic Freedom Index: N/A
Structure of employment rate (Aged 15–64):

Cultural social facts:
Religion: Muslims, Christians, Druze
Internet usage: 6,025,631 (2017)
Internet penetration: 32.6%

Syrian culture puts a large emphasis on family, religion, and self-improvement. Syrian society is quite hierarchical, and people tend to adhere to the stratifications between social statuses. A person's wealth, education, and professionalism are the biggest class indicators.

Comparison of mobile/smartphone usage per 100 population in countries of meritocratic system

Country	Mobile/Smartphone Usage
US	120.7
Canada	86.5
Mexico	88.5
UK	119.5
France	106.2
Germany	133.6
Ireland	102.9
Italy	141.3
Netherlands/Holland	120.5

Japan	135.5
South Korea	124.9
India	87.3
Pakistan	73.4
Singapore	146.8
Malaysia	133.9
Indonesia	164.9
Australia	112.7
New Zealand	136.0
Egypt	105.5
Israel	126.7
Brazil	113.0
Chile	127.5
Peru	121.0
Argentina	139.8
South Africa	156.0

Source: EIU—2021 Statistics

Comparison of mobile/smartphone usage per 100 population in countries of monocratic system

Country	Mobile/Smartphone Usage
China	

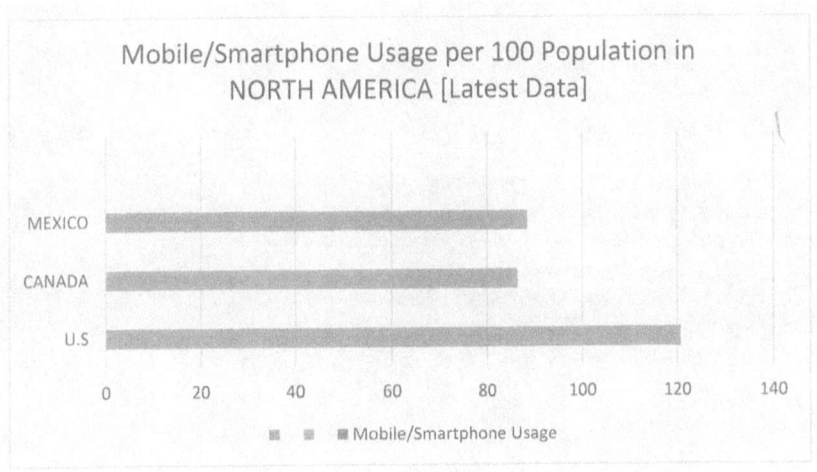

Source: EIU-2020 Statistics

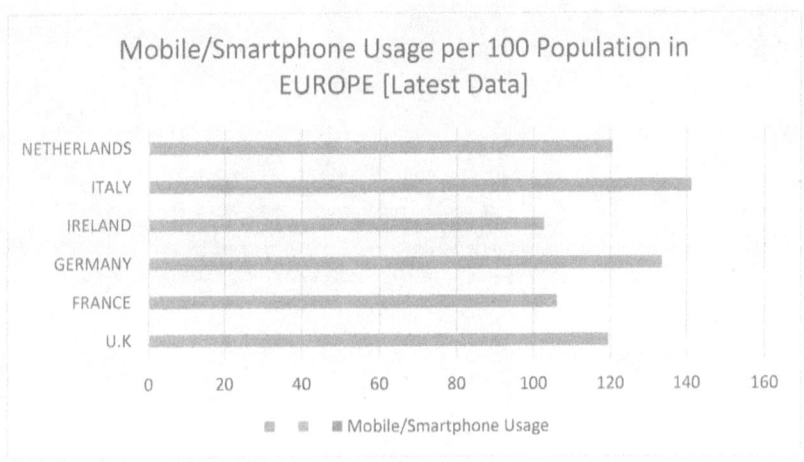

Source: EIU-2020 Statistics

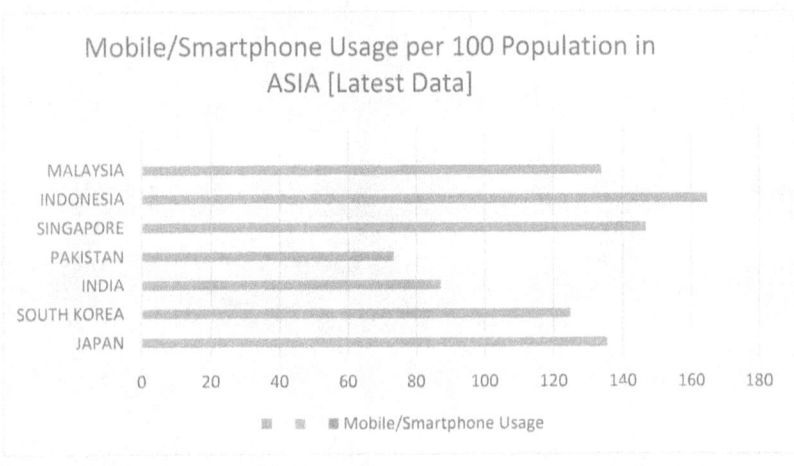

Source: EIU-2020 Statistics

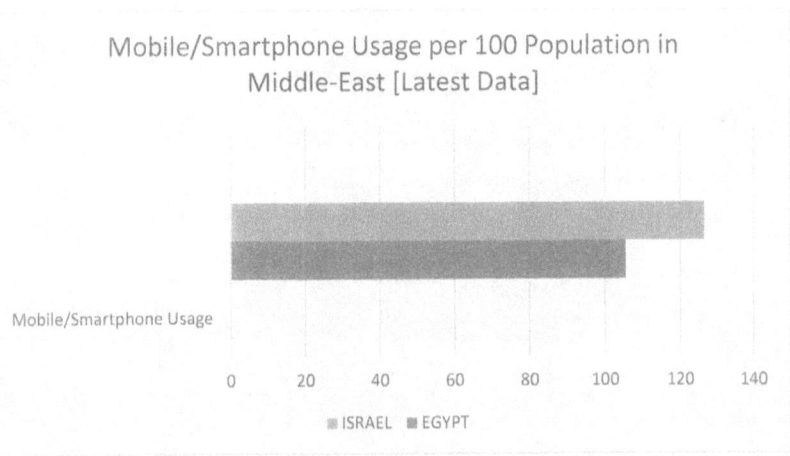

Source: EIU-2020 Statistics

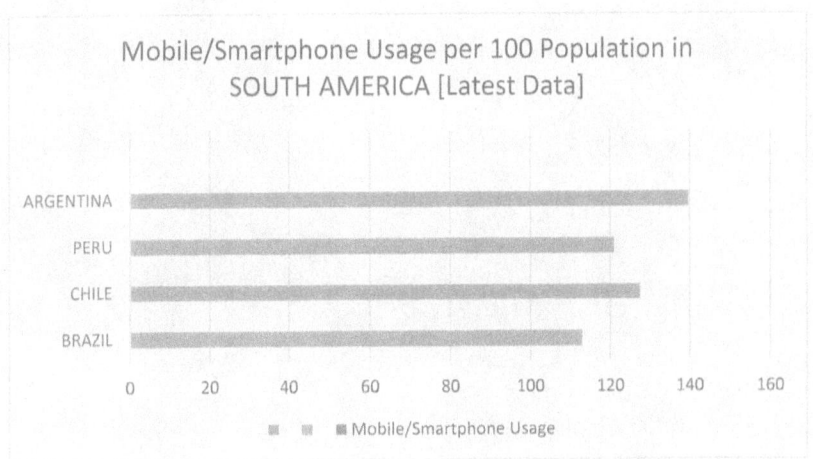

Source: EIU-2020 Statistics

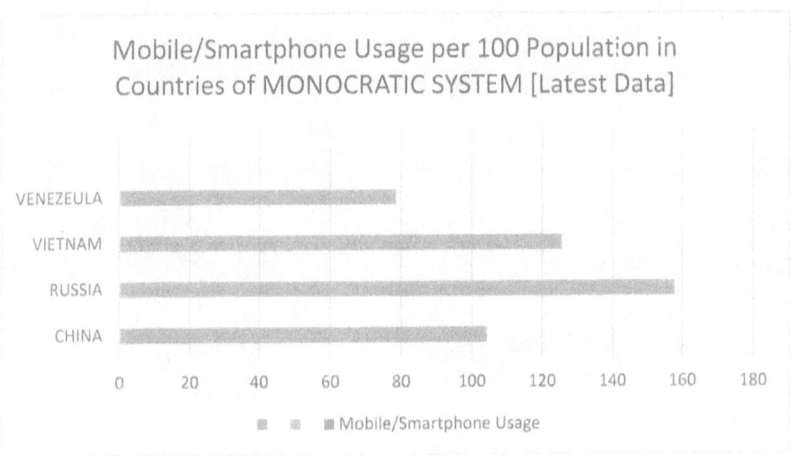

Source: EIU-2020 Statistics

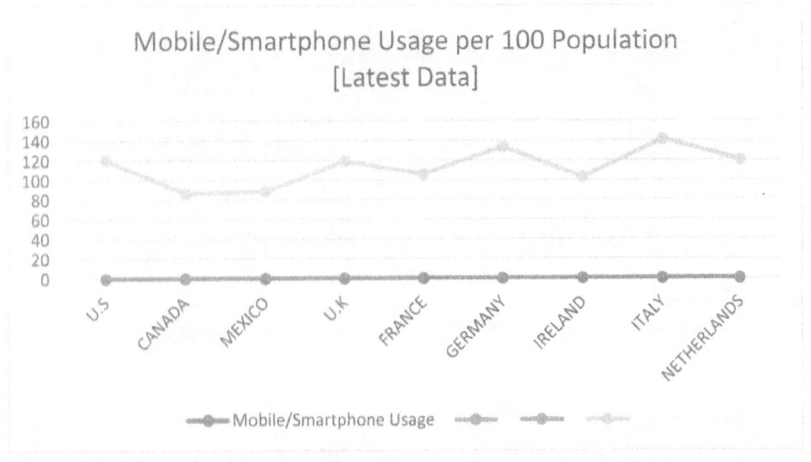

Source: EIU-2020 Statistics

Vietnam   125.6
Venezeula   78.5

Source: EIU—2021 Statistics

CHAPTER 7

GLOBAL MARKETING RESEARCH

Global marketing research is systematic gathering, recording, and analysis of qualitative/quantitative data about marketing products/ services in the global marketplace. Therefore, systematic planning is required at all phases of the global marketing process. Consumers/ customers in global marketplace have different customers/cultures and cultural sensitivity. Basic cultural and market intelligence information will be needed to maximize the marketing research effectiveness. The global marketing research involves information required to address the issues, designing the research methods in gathering information, executing, and implementing the data gathering process. Thereafter, the data gathered has to be analyzed and interpreted and presented to the global marketing management for decision-making. The purpose of marketing research is to furnish the management with relevant accurate, reliable, valid, and up-to-date market information.

Market research and marketing research are reciprocally related to each other. Market research is an exploration of the size, characteristics (population, age, education, workforce, literacy rate, health, GDP, religion, language etc.) and potential of a country/market;

whereas marketing research is gathering and analysis of information about the moving of goods/services from producers to consumers of the country/market from the market analysis which yields information from market research. Conducting global marketing research is an important first step in doing business in another country. Prior to going into another country, we need to understand that country's economic and cultural landscapes, utilizing secondary data available from various sources, including government statistics and publications from industry and trade associations. Global marketing research is conducted either simultaneously or separately to facilitate marketing decisions in more than one country.

The global marketing research process involves the trade disciplines as usual marketing research, but there are some differences. Namely, the national differences between countries arising out of cultural, economic, and social differences. The global marketing researchers in the twenty-first century and beyond will be influenced by several factors such as Internet/communication technology, big data, and digitalization. In brief, gathering data in far corners of the globe plays a crucial role for decision making by the management. Therefore, global market/marketing researchers for the twenty-first century and beyond has got to be well-trained with strong research skills. In other words, he/she has to have adequate skills in computing together with a strong know-how approach in statistics and excellent communication skills to the relevant management.

The decision making on global marketing strategy is based usually upon information about individual country's market potential, requirements of customers, market trends, competitors' behavior, segmentation of the market, and products/services. Global marketing strategies are clearly specified at the corporate level with financial resources in their minds. The main role of global market/marketing researchers is to gather more market information. The following queries that global marketing researchers should ask—the reason for the research rather the purpose of the research and what research should be done; outline the research; company's long-term objectives in the global economy; the budget and market data needed for marketing strategy; how the market data is obtained; research design and data analysis.

Road map for global market/marketing research: Global market/marketing research process

Expansion of bigger *market* share opportunity in *global market* to
Need of *information* through global market/marketing research to
Country/multi-countries > *global* to
Gathering *secondary data* to
Gathering *primary data* > *research design* to
Data analysis to
Interpretation/presentation of findings

The initial phase of the global market/marketing research process is to understand the purpose for the research. The purpose must understand the opportunities that arise or expect the problems that are encountered or predicted. Management must also assess any alternatives, and the results to be utilized in decision-making by the management. For example, expansion of bigger market share. The next phase of the research process is to set apart any real issue that needs to be engaged in using the data to solve the problem. The following phase of the research process is to decide on the information required by the company for decision-making on global digital economy. For example, the company may decide to go globally by expanding bigger market share opportunity, exporting merchandise to the target market. There are a number of options available to companies for global marketing.

Secondary research helps in extenuating the pressure off gathering primary data. Primary data research has to be undertaken in all the countries that have been selected for global market/marketing research. The objective of primary research is to gather data from research instruments, and the collection of data has to be decided depending upon the country's information and its cultural difference, geographical limitation, and language barriers. Since the cost of gathering of primary data is enormous global market/marketing, researchers should gather preliminary data on an individual country prior to collecting actual data.

When it comes to primary research, exploratory research is used widely in global market/marketing research as it is more inexpensive and economical in terms of money and time. On the other hand, descriptive research requires a large quantity of data. It focuses on contributing a description of the existing market phenomenon. Global market/marketing researchers utilize descriptive research to look for similarities and difference among markets which will help in formulating market strategy. Exploratory research focuses on qualitative rather than quantitative data collection. This helps the global market/marketing researcher for prompt answers to the problem on hand. Exploratory research is most relevant when the primary objective is to identify the problem, to define the problem more accurately, or explore the possibility of alternative courses of action. Exploratory research can accommodate in formulating hypotheses regarding problems or opportunities.

There are numerous ways to gather data via survey methods: namely, personal interview, telephone interview, mail survey, and online/Internet survey. In global market/marketing research, the selection of specific survey method is difficult because of the difference in technological developments in different countries. Personal interview is the most effective flexible form of gathering data. This interview is a one-to-one encounter, and this makes the respondent at ease. The researcher has to put a lot of effort in winning the confidence of the respondent. The global market/marketing researcher conducting the survey has to have basic requirements: namely, understanding of the research project, know-how of the industry, familiarity with the country's cultural traits, and the language of the region.

Telephone interviews are being used extensively in global market/marketing research. In most regions of the world, telephone/smartphone interviews are conducted because of the advanced technology. Mail survey is a method where a questionnaire is mailed to potential respondents who complete/fill the survey or feedback with answers. Mail surveys are commonly used in countries where literacy rate is high. Mail surveys are difficult as there won't be current mailing lists available, although mailing lists can be obtained from country's telephone directories and commercial sources available.

The length of the questionnaire, the content, layout, format, the method of addressing the respondents, cover letter, the type of return envelope, and postage are to be considered in mail surveys.

Online/Internet surveys are transforming the character of global market/marketing research. The advantages of Internet/online marketing research surveys are as follows:

- Internet/online marketing research surveys have the capability of being enhanced through the use of graphics, audio/video.

- Internet/online marketing research resurveys can be personalized in that respondents can be asked only pertinent questions, being able to pause and then resume the survey research as needed.

- Distribution of marketing research surveys to tens of thousands of people around the globe is completed with a click of a mouse button.

- With respect to completion rates, accuracy, Internet/online marketing research surveys are the most successful.

- Internet/online marketing research surveys, whether conducted through e-mails/websites, generate greater response accuracy by reducing response error, interviewer bias, information processing mistakes, and sampling distribution problems.

- Quicker turnaround for Internet/online marketing research surveys.

The methodologies for conducting online/web surveys are very similar to those used for traditional research surveys. One of the important issues for global marketing researchers when developing a study in the choosing an appropriate "data gathering method."

Questions they ask themselves include the following:

- What is the most direct and cost-effective means of reaching the targeted sample/audience?

- What methodology will give forth the most representative sample for the survey?
- Objectives of the research must be defined, considering the characteristics of the audience that the researcher going to conduct survey for.
- Identify the target/audience who has the online/Internet access,
- Designing the survey instrument/questionnaire,
- Invite people to participate via email, and
- Monitor the findings/results.

Online/Internet surveys have huge advantages over the traditional survey methods in terms of high quality, turnaround time, and money. In other words, online/web research surveys offer advantages including cost-effectiveness, quicker in response. Internet and social media have connected the global community. These have emerged as a reliable source for global marketing research, and with such an active growth pattern around the globe, the global market/marketing researchers are employing this medium for their survey needs. Mobile/smartphone technology plays a vital role in global market/marketing research surveys. Advancement and growth in Internet and mobile technology has impacted the collection of data.

Global market/marketing research project in a nutshell

Firms/companies need to commence with the perception that they are working in a global digital economy, that globalization and digitalization are an essential business strategy that every multinational company must follow, and that know-how of the global market landscape is crucial. They also need to understand the distinction between global studies and multi-country studies. Companies also must adhere to research project design appropriately for the country as well as to practice cultural sensitivity in all *phases* of a project. Culture and infrastructure that differs in every country significantly influences research project design. Data gathering and choice of methodology, too, may have limited choices. Even questionnaire/

survey questions have to be localized in accordance with the selection of sampling.

Phase 1: Planning. When planning a global market/marketing research project, timing the project is the most vital part of it. Everyone involved in the project must understand that any project related problems—particularly those that have an impact on cost/timing—must be communicated immediately.

Stick to schedule, timing, and budgets.

Establish communications procedure and coordination with suppliers/clients (e-mail/voicemail).

Phase 2: Execution. The execution phase, if careful planning and a proper design have been put into place, can be relatively problem-free. However, issues might arise that often could have been resolved at the outset.

What are the local nuances in respondent availability, sample, lists, maps, field execution, and quality control?

What is the language translation?

Phase 3: Project design. It has to be appropriate for the country.

Choose survey methodology.

Phase 4: Quality control.

Immense care is needed to obtain the right information.

Phase 5: Data analysis and interpretation. Interpretation has to be made from cultural perspectives.

CHAPTER 8

SURVEY RESEARCH: DESIGNING QUESTIONNAIRE/INSTRUMENT AND SAMPLING

Survey research plays a crucial role in global market/marketing research. In other words, survey research is an important source of information for global market/marketing research, and questionnaire/survey instruments are used to gather information through surveys. The key issue is the development of a questionnaire that is clear, easily comprehensible, and easy to administer. Questionnaires make it possible for the global market/marketing researcher to quantify all aspects of the research that are being analyzed and interpreted.

The following factors are to be considered when designing questionnaires:

- The respondent should understand the questions in the questionnaire.
- The respondent should possess enough knowledge to answer the questions in the questionnaire.

- The respondent should be willing to participate without any external pressure.
- Questions need to be articulated so as to collect the desired information from respondents and to evade miscommunication between the researcher and the respondent.
- In global market/marketing research surveys, questionnaires need to be designed to minimize potential sources of biased answers, and this can appear instantly as a result of the questionnaire itself and the topic covered in it. The biased answer can arise from the interaction between the researcher and the respondent. The biased answer also can crop up from the characteristics of the respondent, such as his/her response style or socioeconomic/cultural/demographic origins.
- The content and format of the questionnaire in which the response is obtained to be meticulously considered. Content refers to the general concept that the question is strived to address whereas format refers to the way of asking this question including the scale type to be used. As mentioned earlier, each question in the questionnaire should be unbiased.
- In global market/marketing research, translation of questionnaire is an important part in the survey research process.
- The research is conducted usually in local language in a particular country. Questionnaires must be prepared in one language and then translated into the language of each country researched.

Responses have to be translated back into the original language for analysis and interpretation. Researchers must bear in mind that idioms/phrases mean different things in different cultures. Logical sequence of questions should be checked prior to pretesting the questionnaire as this is an important stage in survey research.

If a global market/marketing researcher needs to gather high quality data, the following tips are needed for questionnaire design:

- Questions in questionnaire/the survey instrument may elicit different feedback if asked via online/telephone/

mobile/smartphone/mail-in-survey/personal survey. Visual design elements have an enormous impact in how questions are read/interpreted in online market/marketing research surveys. Care must be taken into account the type of questions in questionnaire that are good fit for online mobile/smartphone research surveys.

- Correct and appropriate *wording* must be adhered when formulating a questionnaire, so it accurately reflects the issue of interest is one of the hardest parts in writing a questionnaire.
- "Logical flow" in the questions plays an important part to evade inconsistencies that could confuse respondents resulting biased answers in feedback.
- "Format of the questions" too plays a crucial part in writing a questionnaire.

Internet/social media has changed the way global market/marketing research is conducted in many regions of the global market landscape. We find that in many of the countries of the meritocratic system such as US, UK, Canada, EU, and Japan, they use online surveys instead of using traditional methods—personal/mail surveys/telephone.

They find online surveys are better than traditional methods for the following reasons:

- Online surveys can be made inciting to engage the respondents while answering the survey.
- The researcher can make the questions more relevant, and the format of online survey is that precise for respondent to answer.
- In online survey, the researcher has flexibility to use the response to design follow-up questions.
- In online survey, a respondent sees first either in the computer or in mobile smartphone is the screen greeting the respondent in enticing manner to response.

- It provides the opportunity to define/describe the purpose of the survey to respondents. The first question sets the tone for the rest of the survey questions in the questionnaire.

Internet/mobile technology is being used widely by consumers around the globe. Therefore, surveys should be mobile compatible, so that respondents get an option of answering questions in the questionnaire while they are on the move. Specific instructions for answering questions in each question should be included. Formats of response play an important role. The response can be in the form of radio button/check boxes/drop-down-menu/rank-order/open-ended text boxes in order to select any of the appropriate for the type of question. Font size and color also have stimulus on the case of reading. In online survey, researchers can include images. Finally, at the end of the survey, include a thank-you note for taking part in the survey.

Points to consider for online survey research

- Emailing letter of invitations, reminder email letters, incentives, and ensuring survey usability are all routine parts of conducting *online* survey research. The letter for inviting survey-respondents plays an important part in *online* surveys. It improves rate of survey response. The invitation letter for *online* surveys should be carefully considered and personalized if possible.
- Reminder email letters are an easy and effective way to increase response rates for *online* surveys. After you have emailed your initial invitation letter, a follow-up email letter should always be sent out to contacts that have *not* taken the survey yet.
- You also can consider an incentive which is reward provided in exchange for completing the survey.
- A well-designed *online* survey is important for engaging with a respondent and providing a user-friendly survey taking experience. Interactive questions are one way

to enhance your *online* survey design to provide a more engaging and user-friendly survey experience.

- Good question wording can improve survey enjoyment of participation.
- Try to evade unnecessary wording. Do not make the respondent read more than they have to.
- Try to avoid leading the respondent. These are phrases that encourage respondents to answer a certain way. This leads to poor data quality since you have biased the respondent's answers.
- Try to evade using technical jargons.

How to design a questionnaire for global market/marketing research

To design a good questionnaire for global market/marketing research, the following factors are to be taken into consideration:

Decide what information is required in order that they are achieved.

A global market/marketing research study objectives are its main and most vital consideration as these objectives drive the research of the marketing research design, the construction of the questionnaire, and the data analytics/interpretation of the data.

Phrasing the questions: make the questions as simple as possible. In other words, each question should be clearly written, in plain English, free of jargon and without ambiguity.

Steer clear of uncommon/sophisticated words. In brief, try to write questions the way you speak, in a conversational manner so that it's easier for respondents to understand the question and answer them, and it may help to keep them interested.

The must be a logical flow in the questionnaire. Question sequence can be vital to the success of global market/marketing research survey. The opening question should be constructed to interest respondents and keep them involved.

Use a scale (for example: Likert Scale) that the respondent can easily understand and use. A scale doesn't have to be symmetric, nor does it have to be equal number of favorable and unfavorable part.

Try to keep your questions close-ended.

The final step is to test the questionnaire.

Sampling

In designing a *sampling* plan for global market/marketing research, the first step is to determine the level at which *sampling* is to be conducted. When a global market/marketing researcher considers a particular country, he/she has to evaluate whether an appropriate *sample* frame for the target-population exists. The following step is to determine the *sampling* methods to be utilized, the overall size of the *sample*, and the relevant *sample* level. In global market/marketing research, differences in market characteristics and the research infrastructure from one country to another country, imply that the development of the *sampling* plan and survey administration procedures may involve more innovative thought and effort. The purpose of global market/marketing research is to study the characteristics and preferences of population. In deciding the appropriate sampling, a number of factors are to be considered. In outlining the sample, a number of different levels may be considered, including the global market, countries/regions, and to evaluate whether an appropriate sample frame for the target population exists. Once the target population to be sampled has been decided, the availability of a list of population elements from which the sample may be drawn should be evaluated. In global context, this presents difficulties due to the scarcity of information available on businesses/industries in other countries.

The market/marketing researchers choose a subset of elements from the population, and this subset is known as sample. From this sample, they make then make a presumption about the population based on the relevant information gathered from the sample. This assumption is that the sampling is representative of the population and data gathered from the sample can be applied to all members of the population. The methods of sampling are probability sampling and non-probability sampling. In probability sampling, each member of the population has a known probability of being chosen. Probability sampling includes simple random sampling, stratified sampling, systematic sampling, cluster sampling, multi-stage sampling; whereas non-probability sampling includes: convenience sampling, judgement sampling, quota sampling, snowball sampling. In many countries including the developing countries, use systematic random sampling. It poses some difficulty due to the lack of sampling lists, street maps, urban development, and scattered rural populations.

CHAPTER 9

SAMPLE OF VARIOUS QUESTIONNAIRES

Exhibit: 1. A mail questionnaire of the marketing managers of companies within Kensington/ Chelsea area of London Borough

Please check (x) your answer.

1. Overall, how would you rate business conditions in Kensington/ Chelsea area?

    ( ) Excellent
    ( ) Good
    ( ) Fair
    ( ) Poor
    ( ) Very poor

2. Would you say Kensington/Chelsea business area is more or less suitable for your business now than it was five years ago?

( ) More suitable
( ) Same
( ) Less suitable
( ) No opinion

3. If past trends continue, would you predict there will be fewer, more, of the same number of companies in Kensington/Chelsea area next year?

( ) Fewer
( ) More
( ) Same

Please indicate your degree of agreements with the comments below. Please circle if you strongly agree, mildly agree, neither agree nor disagree, or strongly disagree.

4. Kensington/Chelsea area is an active shopping/retail center.

Strongly Agree
Mildly Agree
Neither Agree nor Disagree
Mildly Disagree
Strongly Disagree

5. The future of Kensington/Chelsea area looks very bright.

Strongly Agree
Mildly Agree
Neither Agree nor Disagree
Mildly Disagree
Strongly Disagree

6. Occupying an office/company in the Kensington/Chelsea are rather than elsewhere in London has more advantages than disadvantages.

    Strongly Agree
    Mildly Agree
    Neither Agree nor Disagree
    Mildly Disagree
    Strongly Disagree

7. Off-street parking in the Kensington/Chelsea area is inadequate.

    Strongly Agree
    Mildly Agree
    Neither Agree nor Disagree
    Mildly Disagree
    Strongly Disagree

8. In the next five years your business will move out of Kensington/ Chelsea area.

    Strongly Agree
    Mildly Agree
    Neither Agree nor Disagree
    Mildly Disagree
    Strongly Disagree

9. The Borough of Kensington is very willing to respond to problems in Kensington/Chelsea are.

    Strongly Agree
    Mildly Agree
    Neither Agree nor Disagree
    Mildly Disagree
    Strongly Disagree

10. What is your business activity?

    ( ) Retail trade
    ( ) Wholesale trade
    ( ) Finance/insurance/real estate
    ( ) Services
    ( ) Transportation
    ( ) Other

11. What was your average number of paid full-time employees in the Kensington/Chelsea are?

12. Please estimate how many of these employees are managerial and how many are non-managerial?

    Number of managerial employees:
    Number of non-managerial employees:

13. What was your average monthly payroll for the company (before deductions) in the Kensington/Chelsea area?

14. What was the distribution of your company's payroll to full-time employees in the Kensington/Chelsea area?

    Yearly Salary/Wage Range (In Pounds Sterling) No. of employees
    Under 10,000

    10,000–19,999

    20,000–29,999

    30,000–39,999

    40,000–49,999

    50,000–59,999

60,000–69,999

70,000 or over

15. Approximately how much office space does your company/business occupy in the Kensington/Chelsea area?

Office space:
Other space:

16. Does your company's operation in the Kensington/Chelsea area generate sales revenue from customers buying within the Kensington/Chelsea area?

( ) YES (Go to Question 17)
( ) No (Go to Question 18)

17. If YES, please estimate your sales volume in Pounds Sterling for the last year from customers buying within Kensington/Chelsea area: Pounds Sterling:

18. In what year did you start operating your company in the Kensington/Chelsea area?

19. Do you intend to invest in capital improvement for expansion or remodeling of your Kensington/Chelsea facility in the next five years?

YES (Go to Question 20)
No (Thank you for completing the questionnaire.)

20. If YES, approximately how much do you intend to invest: Pounds Sterling?

Thank you very much for your cooperation. Please return the completed questionnaire in the postage-paid envelope at your earliest convenience.

Exhibit 2. A mail questionnaire for customers of Investment Times

Please indicate your answer choice by placing (x) in the appropriate box Please put an (x) in the box for all that apply:

Which of the following statements best describe why you read The London *Financial Times*?

To follow general news of the economy/finance ( )
To follow stock/securities I own or am interested in ( )
I enjoy reading financial news around the world ( )
To read the personal finance/investing coverage ( )
To follow information about my company/competitors/cus-
    tomers ( )
To help plan future career/business opportunities ( )

How often do you read the following news columns in the London *Financial Times*?

	Weekly	Sometimes	Never
Personal Technology	( )	( )	( )
Intrinsic Value	( )	( )	( )
Banks/Financial Institutions	( )	( )	( )

How often do you read one or more times on investments/real estate/insurance?

	Investment	Real Estate	Insurance
Every week	( )	( )	( )
Twice a month	( )	( )	( )
At least once a month	( )	( )	( )
Never	( )	( )	( )

Who paid your subscription to London *Financial Times*?

> I paid for it myself ( )
> My company paid for it ( )
> It was a gift subscription ( )

Which of the following print products do you currently subscribe to at home or at work?

> *The Asian Wall Street Journal* Weekly ( )
> *MoneyWeek* ( )
> *The Hedge Fund Journal* ( )
> *Euromoney* ( )
> EU Bank Journal ( )
> *Wall Street Journal* Weekly ( )
> Other   (Please specify)

When you are traveling or away from the office or home (for business or personal reasons), do you purchase any of the following publications at the location listed below?

	Financial Times	Asian Wall Street Journal
At an airport	( )	( )
At a train /bus station	( )	( )
At a hotel	( )	( )
Other type of newsstand	( )	( )
Vending machine	( )	( )
Tesco/Sainsbury's/Asda/Waitrose/Lidl	( )	( )
Other retail store	( )	( )
Do not purchase	( )	( )

Which of the following products/services do you personally use at home or at work?

	Home	Work
Stocks/Bonds/other online service	( )	( )
Money and Investing Update (Internet)	( )	( )
Other	( )	( )

About you and your business or profession:

What is the nature of your employer's primary business?

If you do not work for an employer, please give your profession or occupational status. (Please be specific: e.g., manufacturing, whole-sale/retail, foods, law firm, dentist, student, homemaker, retired, living from investments

What is your title or position? (Please specify):

Do you work primarily from?
Home ( )   Outside your home ( )

Please indicate if your work involved decisions in any of the following areas for your company? (Please mark (X) in the box for all that apply.)

Advertising	( )
Marketing/sales	( )
Bank services	( )
Financial services	( )
Insurance	( )
Computers, software/hardware	( )
Office equipment	( )

Telecommunications equipment/services   ( )

Research and development   ( )

Medical equipment/services   ( )

Freight or transportation services ( )

Industrial machinery/building materials   ( )

Other ( )   (Please specify)

How many employees are there in your entire firm—that is, the total number of employees including all plants, divisions, branches, and subsidiaries throughout the world?

( ) Fewer than 25
( ) 25–99
( ) 100–249
( ) 250–499
( ) 500–999
( ) 1,000–2,499
( ) 2,500–4,999
( ) 5,000–9,999
( ) 10,000 or more

About your international business:

Do you or are you involved in the decision making or operations of such business for your company outside the United Kingdom?

( ) Yes
( ) No

In which areas of the world do you or your company currently conduct business/or plan to conduct business in the next 12 months?

Please mark (X) in the box for all that apply.

( ) Asia/Pacific Rim
( ) Canada
( ) Middle East/Africa
( ) Mexico
( ) South America/Central America
( ) EU
( ) Eastern Europe
( ) Russia
( ) Other:

How often do you contact via Internet/online, mobile/telephone, fax or send overnight?

Packages outside United Kingdom?

	Internet/online	Mobile/telephone	Fax
Daily	( )	( )	( )
Weekly	( )	( )	( )
Monthly	( )	( )	( )
Quarterly	( )	( )	( )
Occasionally	( )	( )	( )
Never	( )	( )	( )

Did you travel for business outside of the United Kingdom in the past year?

( ) Yes
( ) No

If yes, how frequently did you travel to the following areas in the past year?

	Asia	EU	South America/ Central America
1–2 round trips	( )	( )	( )
3–5	( )	( )	( )
6–11	( )	( )	( )
12 or more	( )	( )	( )

About business/home electronic use:

Do you use a laptop/desktop/personal computer?

( ) Yes at home
( ) Yes at work
( ) No

If you own or have access to laptop computer, how often do you travel with it?

( ) Almost always
( ) Often
( ) Occasionally
( ) Never

About other publications/media:

Please mark (X) in the box for all that apply.

( ) *The Economist*
( ) *Fortune*
( ) *Forbes*
( ) Trade publications
( ) *Businessweek*
( ) Other

Which of the following IT services do you personally use at home or at work?

( ) Google
( ) Bing
( ) Yahoo
( ) Other

Which of the following types of news and information have you used the above IT information services for in the last month?

( ) General news
( ) Business news
( ) Financial news
( ) Stock/bond
( ) Travel/weather information
( ) Sports
( ) Other:

About your investments:

Which of the following types of investments/assets do you or other members of your household currently own?

( ) Common/preferred stocks

How much time do you spend monitoring and tracking your investments in a week?

( ) Under one hour
( ) One to under four hours
( ) Four to under seven hours
( ) Seven to under ten hours
( ) Ten hours or more

Which of the following do you currently consult for advice on your personal investment?

Please mark (X) in the box for all that apply.

( ) Investment Advisory Service/Online services etc.
( ) Financial planner
( ) Accountant
( ) Lawyer
( ) Stockbroker
( ) Myself

About you and your household:

Are you:

( ) Male
( ) Female

What is your marital status?

( ) Married
( ) Single
( ) Divorced or separated
( ) Widowed

What is the highest level of education you have attained?

( ) High school or less
( ) Attended college
( ) Graduated from college
( ) B.A/BSc
( ) M.A/MSc
( ) PhD/MD

Thank you for completing the questionnaire.

Exhibit 3. A mail questionnaire for Traveler's/Leisure Card members

Please mark (X) in the appropriate box.

What is your Gender?

    ( ) Male
    ( ) Female

How many domestic leisure trips do you expect to take this year?

    ( ) 0
    ( ) 1
    ( ) 2
    ( ) 3
    ( ) 4
    ( ) 5 or more

What is the average length of stay for your domestic trips?

    ( ) overnight
    ( ) weekend
    ( ) week-long
    ( ) ten days
    ( ) more than ten days

Do you have a current UK passport?

    ( ) Yes
    ( ) No

How many overseas leisure trips do you expect to take this year?

( ) 0
( ) 1
( ) 2
( ) 3 or more

What is the average length of stay for your overseas trips?

( ) weekend
( ) week-long
( ) 8–14 days
( ) more than 2 weeks

While on vacation, which destination do you prefer?

( ) a destination that is quiet, restful, and relaxing
( ) a destination that has lots of activities
( ) a destination that is known for its cuisine
( ) a destination that is known for its historical significance

Mark (X) three (3) activities you enjoy doing the most when traveling to overseas/domestic location:

( ) Go shopping
( ) Play tennis
( ) Golf
( ) Hiking
( ) Jogging
( ) Bicycling
( ) Sailing
( ) Skiing
( ) Scuba
( ) Swim/beach
( ) Visit vineyards
( ) Visit art galleries

( ) Go to museum
( ) Watching sports/cricket/soccer/hockey
( ) Meet with locals
( ) Go to restaurants
( ) Take in the local night life
( ) Explore surroundings on my own
( ) Visit sites of religious significance
( ) Discover exotic flora and fauna
( ) Drive through countryside
( ) View local architecture
( ) Visit popular tourist attractions

Mark (X) all that apply.

( ) I have taken a cruise
( ) I have ridden on the Orient Express
( ) I have gone on a Safari
( ) I have taken a helicopter sightseeing tour
( ) I have taken a vacation at an all-inclusive resort

Do you use the Internet to preview your destination?

( ) Yes
( ) No

Do you use the Internet to book your travel?

( ) Yes
( ) No

Do you take advantage of last-minute deals on air fares, hotels and car rentals?

( ) Yes
( ) No

What is your favorite destination for domestic travel?

What is your favorite destination for overseas travel?

What is the destination of your next vacation, overseas or domestic?

Thank you for taking the time to complete and return this questionnaire.

Exhibit 4. A mail questionnaire of public perception of economic growth of Brunswick— inner city in Melbourne, Australia

Please read each question carefully and mark (X) on the box that indicates your answer.

1. Brunswick, the inner city's economy is sustainable and competitive and resilient. Your answers will be treated confidentially.

2. To what extent do you agree or disagree that the vision described above is appropriate?

    ( ) Strongly Agree
    ( ) Agree
    ( ) Neither agree nor disagree
    ( ) Disagree
    ( ) Strongly Disagree
    ( ) Don't know

3. Do you have any comments about the vision for economic growth in Brunswick-inner city?

    a. People have access to better-paid and more secure satisfying employment.

b. The local workforce possesses the skills and knowledge they require for work and has access to training to gain new skills.

c. Brunswick—inner city will be widely recognized as a great place to live, work, and visit.

4. To what extent do you agree or disagree that above outcomes are the right ones as the main focus of activities for the future?

( ) Strongly agree
( ) Agree
( ) Neither agree nor disagree
( ) Disagree
( ) Strongly disagree
( ) Don't know

5. Do you have any comments about the outcome?

Our key economic strengths are as follows:
Our large health care sector
Our strong enterprise cultures
Our skilled workforce
Our opportunity sectors
Do you have any comments on how this should be done?

6. Please rank the following in order of how important you think they are in supporting Brunswick-inner city's economic growth, with number one being the most important and number five being the least important.

( ) Encouraging entrepreneurs and supporting stat-ups
( ) Helping our larger businesses to become more resilient to market changes
( ) Strengthening local supply chains to ensure that the overall local economy is more resilient
( ) Improving our infrastructure to enable the economy to grow

( ) Developing our skills base to match business need in Brunswick—inner city, including creating more apprenticeships

7. To what extent you agree or disagree that restaurants/fast-food restaurants are an opportunity sector in Brunswick—inner city?

( ) Strongly Agree
( ) Agree
( ) Neither agree nor disagree
( ) Disagree
( ) Strongly disagree
( ) Don't know

8. To what extent do you agree or disagree that landowners are an opportunity sector in Brunswick inner city?

( ) Strongly agree
( ) Agree
( ) Neither agree nor disagree
( ) Disagree
( ) Strongly disagree
( ) Don't know

9. To what extent do you agree or disagree that businesses are an opportunity sector in Brunswick inner city?

( ) Strongly agree
( ) Agree
( ) Neither agree nor disagree
( ) Disagree
( ) Strongly disagree
( ) Don't know

10. Do you have any additional comments about where the focus for Brunswick inner city's emerging economic growth plans should be?

Thank you for completing the questionnaire.

Exhibit 5. A mail demographic market research questionnaire for Canadians living in various provinces

Which province of Canada do you live?

Mark (X) in appropriate box

( ) Alberta
( ) British Columbia
( ) Manitoba
( ) New Brunswick
( ) Newfoundland and Labrador
( ) Ontario
( ) Quebec
( ) Northwest Territories
( ) Nunavut

Which city of Canada do you live?

( ) Toronto
( ) Vancouver
( ) Montreal
( ) Calgary

Household income:

What was your total household income before taxes during the past 12 months? Mark (X) in appropriate box.

( ) Less than $25,000

( ) $25,000 to $34,999
( ) $35,000 to $49,999
( ) $50,000 to $74,000
( ) $75,000 to $99,999
( ) $100,000 to $149,999
( ) $150,000 or more

What is your ethnicity/race?

African	( )
American	( )
Asian/ Indian	( )
Chinese	( )
Eskimo	( )
European	( )
Hispanic	( )
Other (Please specify)	( )

What is your age?

( ) 18 to 24 years
( ) 25 to 34 years
( ) 35 to 44 years
( ) 45 to 54 years
( ) 55 to 64 years
( ) Age 65 or older

What is your education level?

( ) High school graduate
( ) Completed some college
( ) Associate's degree
( ) Bachelor's degree
( ) Completed some postgraduate
( ) Master's degree

( ) PhD, Law, or Medical degree
( ) Other advanced degree beyond Master's degree

What is the higher degree or level of education you have completed?

( ) Less than high school
( ) High school graduate
( ) Some college, no degree ( ) associate's degree
( ) Bachelors' degree ( ) Master's degree
( ) PhD
( ) Law Degree
( ) Medical degree
( )Professional degree

What is your marital status?

( ) Single
( ) Married
( ) Separated
( ) Widowed
( ) Divorced

What is your gender?

( ) Male
( ) Female

How many hours per week do you usually work at your job?

( ) 35 hours a week or more
( ) Less than 35 hours a week
( ) I am not currently employed

Counting all locations where your employer operates, what is the total number of employees who work there?

( ) 1
( ) 2–9
( ) 10–24
( ) 25–99
( ) 100–499
( ) 500–999
( ) 1000–4,999
( ) 5,000+

What best describes the type of company/organization you work for?

( ) For profit
( ) Non-profit (Religious, arts, social assistance etc.)
( ) Health Care
( ) Education
( ) Other (Please specify)

What level of decision-making authority do you have on purchasing IT related hardware/software?

( ) Final decision-making authority
( ) Significant decision-making or influence
( ) Minimal decision-making or influence
( ) No input

Which of the following most closely matches your job title?

( ) Intern
( ) Entry level
( ) Analyst/Associate
( ) Manager
( ) Senior Manager
( ) Director

( ) Vice-President
( ) Senior Vice-President
( ) Chief Information Officer
( ) Chief Technical Officer
( ) Chief Operating Officer
( ) Chief Marketing Officer
( ) President
( ) Chief Executive Officer
( ) Owner

Thank you for completing the questionnaire.

CHAPTER 10

DATA ANALYSIS IN GLOBAL MARKET/MARKETING RESEARCH

Data analysis in global market/marketing research is the phase when qualitative/quantitative data is brought together and scrutinized in order to draw conclusions based on the data. In other words, data analysis is a process of obtaining data with the objective of discovering useful information for decision-making by marketing management/market/marketing research professionals.

Data analysis involves objectives, relationship, decision-making, and ideas in addition to working with the actual data itself. Once the data has been gathered, the next phase is the choice of appropriate methods and procedure for data analysis. In global market/marketing research, the issues become more complex due to the existence of multiple units of analysis. That said, global market/marketing research data analysis is more complicated due to the hierarchical/multi-characteristics of the design of the survey. Several analyses can be utilized during the initial data analysis phase namely, univariate statistics (for single variable), bivariate associations (correlation), and graphical techniques (for scatter plots).

It is vital to consider the measurement levels of the variables into account for the analyses, as special statistical techniques.

Nominal and ordinal variables: frequency counts (number and percentages); associations cross tabulations, hierarchical loglinear analysis, loglinear analysis, exact tests, computation of near variables.

Continuous variables—distribution: include statistics, median/ standard deviation/variance. In the main data analyses stage, analyses aimed at answering the research question are performed, and any other relevant analysis needed to write the research report.

Let us look into data analysis in the context of market/marketing research. Data preparation and analysis phase includes the editing, coding, transcription, and verification of data. Verification ensures that the data from the original questions have been accurately transcribed. Then each feedback of questions is inspected/edited, and the quality and reliability of the data gathered must be examined. The data from the questions are transcribed and inputted into computer. It is very important to store all data gathered in a database in a single location. It is also necessary to retain the original response/feedback and give identification number for each one to cross-check at the editing phase. Editing of data is done to find any omissions, errors, ambiguities in responses in survey feedback from respondents. Data coding is important as the description of data has name of variable (format of the variable—data/text, etc.), location of the variable in the database, the identification of the feedback sheet.

Once data gathered has been coded, edited, and the quality and the reliability of the data evaluated, and also various sources of bias identified, the next phase is to conduct the data analysis. Various different procedures can be used such as univariate/bivariate/multivariate analysis depending on the number of variables that have to be analyzed. Analyzed data gives meaning to the information that has been gathered. Univariate methods (simplest form of statistical analysis) are utilized for analysis data when there is a single measurement of each element/unit in the sample. Multivariate methods utilized for analyzing data when there are two or more measurements on each element and the variables are analyzed simultaneously.

Univariate and bivariate data analysis can be utilized to test the significance of difference—relative to one or two variables—between two samples. These analyses are descriptive than inferential, and this is performed during the initial phases to identify areas when similarities/differences exist. With the use of descriptive statistics, it is possible to obtain cross-tabulations for two variables. The purpose of crosstabulation is to uncover interrelationships among the variables. Also, where cross-tabulations have been performed, chi-square test can be conducted, and this is a technique for determining the probability that differences between the expected and observed number of cases in each cell are significant. In brief, chi-square test is used to test the statistical independence of two variables. Statistical independence implies that knowledge of value of the other variable. In global market/marketing research, t-tests have been used to test whether the differences in social/cultural status characteristics within two countries of exist. Analysis of variance (ANOVA) can be used to test for the significance of difference between different samples. Regression analysis also can be used. Regression analysis is one of several techniques for assessing and illustrating the general tendencies of movement between two sets of data. In marketing research, the most common application of the techniques is to evaluate data in which one element is that of time and to allow some rough extrapolation of the data towards a forecast of future relationships. There are two types of regression analysis namely, simple regression and multiple regression analysis. In simple regression analysis, the dependent variable is assumed to depend upon a single independent variable whereas in multiple regression analysis, a number of variables are assumed to underlie variance in the dependent variable. In cross-national/country research, multiple regression analysis can be done to evaluate the extent to which certain variables account for variations in one variable within countries, and the results compared from one country to another by statistical testing.

In global market/marketing research, discriminant analysis too can be used to identified which variables are significantly different between two or more national/country samples or unit of analysis. In global market/marketing research, conjoint analysis can be used to examine buying/purchasing preferences for evaluation with regard to different product/service attributes in different countries. These preferences can be compared among counties to evaluate difference and similarities. In global market/marketing research, cluster analysis has been used to group countries into clusters that re similar in certain characteristics. These clusters have been developed based on countries' per capita income, population, import/export, level of literacy rate etc. Factor analysis also has been used in global market/marketing research to reduce the number of variables to be analyzed, and to identify comparable constructs to be compared in subsequent stages of the analysis. The purpose of factor analysis is to simplify massive amounts of data. In global market/marketing research, multidimensional scaling can be used to analyze similarities and differences among countries. It can be used to develop mapping of countries based upon perceived similarities in characteristics such as meritocratic and monocratic systems or even sociocultural characteristics.

In short, data analysis of data collected starts with tabulating data and obtaining descriptive statistics. Prior to tabulating data, data preparation involves logging the data, checking for accuracy, editing, entering the data into the computer, transforming the data, developing and documenting the database. Once data have been edited/checked, they are then ready for analysis. There are two types of analysis. Initially, data that are to be analyzed country-wise and then analyzed comparatively differences across countries. Then univariate and bivariate techniques-chi-square and t-test and multivariate techniques-regression and discriminant analysis, (ANOVA) analysis of covariance, clustering, factor analysis, and multidimensional scaling can be done. Multivariate techniques can be used in all phases when marketing management encounters marketing problems.

It is important to check the quality and validity of the data gathered, prior to conducting quantitative analysis. All data to be scrutinized for possible sources of bias, and differences among countries. The reliability of data from different countries should also be scrutinized and tested and compared from one country to another.

The last phase in data analysis in global market/marketing research is the presentation of the summary report. The entire survey of global market/marketing research project has to be documented in comprehensive format as a written report. The report should include results and major findings, interpretation, and recommendation. The report has to be presented to the management for decision-making process.

CHAPTER 11

GLOBAL MARKET/MARKETING RESEARCH SURVEY TIPS AND ANALYSIS USING SPSS SOFTWARE

SPSS (Statistical Package for the Social Science) is used voluminously by global market/marketing researchers for analysis of survey research data. Global market/marketing researchers can analyze data because it gives you the statistical depth needed to solve a variety of research problems. It provides statistical functions such as descriptive statistics, frequencies, correlation, linear regression, cluster factor analysis, discriminant analysis, and so on. It also provides solutions for data management and data documentation. It is an extremely powerful tool for manipulating and deciphering survey data. SPSS 23/25 Version offers a broad range of statistical and analytical capacities such as planning and data preparation, reporting. The above-mentioned features of SPSS statistical software can be accessed via pull-down menus. It also handles complex data manipulation and analyzes.

Descriptive statistics of SPSS include the following:

- Cross-tabulation
- Bivariate statistics
  o Means
  o t-tests
  o ANOVA
  o Correlation
- Factor analysis
- Cluster analysis
- Discriminant analysis
- Linear regression analysis
- SPSS Version: 25.0 include the following:
  o (Bayesian Statistical function)
  o Linear regression
  o ANOVA
  o t-tests (independence sample)
  o One-sample
  o Pair-sample
  o Binomial Proportion Inference
  o Poisson Distribution analysis
  o P-Pearson Correlation
  o Loglinear Models (to test the independence of two categorical variables)

Author's suggestion to help global market/marketing researcher save time and money as he/she plans, develops, and executes his/her research surveys: first, understand the reason(s) and background for your survey. In other words, define the mission/motivation of your survey. If your company wants to develop your survey's mission, you can use those reason(s) to develop your survey's mission. Once you developed, you can refer to your mission throughout the survey whenever you get stuck. Thereafter, outline your research—develop a plan to implement your mission. Be prepared to know which statistics to run, what initial relationships and patterns you expect to find. Then, you need to consider population before you can develop questions (*questionnaire*) and format your survey. The age of respondents in your population affects the ability to pay attention or their capacity to understand your questions in the questionnaire. Consider gender because phrasing in the question is directed at the right audience and is not offensive.

Determining your sample size will help you decide which type of survey to use. Consider budget and other resources whether you can have sufficient means for a large enough sample size to attain useful results. There are software tools that enable you to determine critical variables (anticipated effect size, confidence, statistical power, and sample size) prior to spending valuable time and resources. Bear in mind that if you have reason to expect a strong effect, then use a smaller sample size. Base the sample size on the minimum adequate sample size of important subgroups in the population. Resolve the appropriate sample size. Once you have determined the size of your sample, you can select the sampling technique that best fits your needs.

There are two basic methods to conducting a survey: self-administered and interviewer-administered methods. Self-administered surveys include mail; interviewer-administered include Internet/online/web and other written surveys, whereas interviewer-administered include telephone and in-person surveys.

Telephone interviewing can be more expensive than other surveys when you consider long-distance phone charges. In-person interviews also incur charges. Mail surveys are more economical if you have a large sample or if your sample spans across a large geographical area. Remember to consider the method of returning the mail survey. For example, including postage on return envelopes can increase expenses but also increase returns. Internet/online/web surveys can also be another cost-effective method.

Internet/online/web surveys can also be challenging on where you decide to conduct them. In US, 75 to 80 percent of population has Internet access. In South American countries, the percentage of Internet access is between 40 to 70, and in China the percentage of Internet access is about 54.3, while in South Korea, it's about 95.1. Using Internet/online/webs surveys, you'll tend to save on postage and printing, and it's easy to analyze the information you've received in an electronic format.

Internet/online/web and telephone surveys are the timeliest method of surveying. The typical time frame for collecting data through Internet/online/web or telephone survey ranges from a few days to a few weeks, while a mailed survey can add at least a month to the process.

If you must ask a lot of questions or expect the respondent to spend an hour or more with your survey, perform in-person surveys. If you can't afford to perform in-person surveys, the second-best option is a self-administered survey. A lengthy mail survey is more likely to be completed than a twenty-minute telephone survey. Prior to choosing a survey type such as Internet/online/web-based, make sure you are able to get a valid sample population with that method. For example, some populations have access to the Internet. However, you cannot assume that everyone has access to the Internet.

The ideal length of your survey is dependent on the population and type of survey. Limit the length of your survey to encourage prospective respondents to participate. Consequently, telephone interviews should run no longer than ten minutes. Face-to-face interviews can continue for an hour or longer. Self-administered surveys should not exceed four pages for most populations. Internet/online/web-based surveys should not require participants to have to take multiple steps to answer each question. With a shorter survey, you should get a higher response rate and reduce the chance of error and missing data. However, you will also get less information from your respondents and may have a less comprehensive study. The key to a successful survey is to ensure that your questions are concise and easy to understand and give you valid and reliable information.

In other words, try to keep each question under twenty-five words, so they remain short and easy to understand. Avoid loaded questions. Try to avoid double-barreled questions such as opinions about two subjects at the same time. Give respondents a way out of answering questions to which they might feel there is a "right" answer. Respondents are more likely to respond if they feel their answer is socially acceptable. Give your respondents a chance to remember. In

135

other words, respondents may have a hard time remembering details about past behavior. Give them time to think back if you are conducting a telephone or in-person survey. Consider using open-ended questions. Open-ended questions can give you a lot of important feedback and details about your respondents. Today, there are techniques available that make above board analysis of open-ended survey responses fast and efficient.

With these tools, open-ended responses help you learn a great deal about your respondents' attitudes, perceptions, and opinions. If your survey is divided into sections, placing open-ended questions and responses at the end of section may give you more flexibility and more room for verbatim responses. There are two types of open-ended questions. With one type of question, you have predetermined list of answers that you expect to receive. Then analyzing responses: you can assign a code for each response instead of typing in each name. You also want to assign codes for answers that you might not have expected. The other type of open-ended question has multiple combination of answers. Coding responses to open-ended questions can be time-consuming and may require data entry personnel who have a good understanding of the subject matter. Also, software tools can automate the tedious tasks involved in coding responses and reduce to hours what used to take so long.

If you provide a scale or choice of answers for the respondent, it's important that the provided answers accurately. The Likert scale is a ranked list of responses, often five or seven, ranging from one pole to an opposite pole. Many researchers include a middle response in a scale. The middle answer offers a comfortable response for subjects who have legitimately divided or neutral opinions. It is important to note that these items are not always "interval-scaled"—meaning, for example, the distance between "strongly agree" and "agree" is the same as "agree" and "neither agree nor disagree." Treating such variables this way can lead to biased statistical results by skewing the weighting of each response.

However, there are statistical packages that can correctly do statistical analysis of such items. Statistical software can help you find and understand patterns in the respondents who answer "Don't know," so you can determine if they share similar characteristics. Statistical software can help you find and understand patterns in the respondents who answer, "I couldn't say" or "Not applicable," so you can determine if they share similar characteristics.

A poorly formatted survey can deter people from responding and can also give skewed results. Make sure you can create an aesthetically pleasing questionnaire that is easy to understand and follow. If you add a space for respondents to make comments, make sure to leave enough room for them to write. The presentation of questionnaire can either encourage or deter a person from responding. Make sure your survey is inviting by: Including plenty of white space so the questionnaire does not appear intimidating using no more than two typefaces.

To ensure that your respondent doesn't get mixed up or obscured at the beginning of a written self-administered survey, tell the respondent what instrument (pen, pencil) to use. At the beginning of each section, give instructions on how to respond to the questions. Also, don't forget to tell the respondent how to return the survey when it's completed. Make it as easy as possible for your respondents to fill out the survey. In other words, put questions in upper and lowercase and responses in bold. Use check boxes rather than blanks. Make it obvious where the respondent is supposed to make marks, so it's easy for respondents to complete the survey.

You shouldn't cut corners by eliminating the trial phase. There will always be problems that can be spotted only through pretesting, and it may be too late to fix them once the survey hits the field. Conduct at least two pretests for all new studies. The first pretest aims to correct problems with the self or interview-administered survey, openly asking for help and comments. Conduct the second pretest as you plan to carry out the actual survey. In a mail survey, go ahead and mail the surveys to a test sample to gauge response time and other factors. Usually, no more than seventy-five respondents are needed for a pretest. The pretest population should be similar in characteristics (not in size) to the population of real survey. When analyzing the responses from a pretest, you may find the following problems: little or no variance among responses; too many "don't know" responses; too many "other" responses; unclear skip patterns; misinterpretation of open-ended questions. If you find these problems, consider the relevance of a question and its wording.

Make special considerations when writing and formatting a telephone survey. Since respondents can't reread items on a page, make sure they understand and remember the question that the interviewer is reading: keep questions short—no more than twenty-five words; offer few response options—no more than five; limit number of items to rank—no more than three.

When writing a script for telephone interview, script the entire call, from the greeting through the closing. Make it clear and direct. You want to make sure the interviewer can easily follow the script, because simple fizzle in speech can affect the confidence your respondents have in your survey and the overall results. Give your respondents a breather. Breaking your survey into sections will hold the respondent's interest longer. Even if there is not a logical subject change, make one. You need to keep respondents interested and alert during a long stretch of questions. During the survey, telephone interviewers must concentrate on talking, listening, and recording responses. To make their job easier and attain more accurate responses, devise a simple coding scheme. In other words, use numbers to record answers when respondents rate something on a scale, so the interviewers don't have to write a long answer.

Make special consideration when planning telephone and in-person interviews. For telephone surveys, give the interviewer a long list of names in case your sample isn't available or is unwilling to participate. To be safe, you should have between seven and fifteen times more names than the number of completed surveys you want. Lack of respondents' availability and lack of cooperation are the main barriers to response for telephone or in-person interviews. To compensate for lack of availability, interviewers must keep calling. As the interviewer, you should keep the introduction concise and not mention the length of the interview unless it is short or if the respondent asks. Also, mention any incentives that the survey offers at the beginning. If the person does not want to participate, don't press, say "Thank you," and move on to the next name.

The following qualities make good interviewers:

- Understands respondents and is empathetic,
- Listens well,
- Maintains attitude of genuine interest,
- Is objective,
- Accepts rejection, and
- Doesn't let mood affect performance.

When special design and notification consideration when distributing written and Internet/online/web-based surveys. To increase response, write a straightforward cover letter—no longer than one page—explaining: the purpose of the survey, the benefits of the respondent's participation, the seriousness/importance of the survey, how the respondent's opinions will be used, and who is sponsoring the survey. If possible, have an important or influential person sign the letter to give the survey more legitimacy. Sending a lengthy survey via certified mail can greatly increase response rate. Email can increase the response rate and timeliness of the return. Try to send respondents an email or postcard—a pre-notification notice—to alert them that the survey will arrive in approximately one week. This notice will increase the likelihood of response because the respondents are more likely to expect or recognize the survey when it arrives. The note may also spark curiosity in the respondents, and they will look for the survey. Commitments cards and commitment emails ask prospective respondents to return a postcard or email agreeing to participate in the survey. Pre-notification notice generally gives a larger response rate than commitment cards or emails. However, commitment cards give you an estimate of the response rate. Send a reminder by postcard or email approximately one or two weeks after the initial survey mailing.

These reminders should thank people who completed the survey while also reminding those who have not yet responded. Send out duplicate surveys to nonrespondents, or to the entire sample group ten to fourteen days after the thank-you and reminder postcard.

Wait about six weeks to start analysis for mail surveys. For Internet/online/web-based surveys, you should expect to receive completed surveys in less than one week. Response rate is an important issue to consider since it can have a great impact on your results. Software can help you analyze missing data patterns and account for these nonresponsive variables.

Analysis delivers the value from your survey data. There are several ways to evaluate your data. After the surveys are returned, always place a unique identification number on each survey record. This unique number, sometimes called a "case ID," will help you track down problems in data cleaning as well as flag case of particular interest during analysis. When examining a new dataset, perform data verification and cleaning. As the analyst, you should have an idea of how your file should look. Using data collection software during this step can help you save time by streamlining the process. Run a series of cross-tabulations before doing further analysis to look for: inconsistent relationships (such as someone saying they are female, but whose relationship to the head of household is "son"), unexpected averages, a large number of missing values.

When performing complex analyses, keep record of the procedures you perform or the way you created new variables. This record will help you reconstruct your analyses if any questions arise when you write the report. Different statistical procedures are appropriate for variables depending on what you want to learn and the level of measurement of the variable. Nominal variables provide a list of choices with no meaningful order to the list. Examples include gender. Use the mode and run frequencies and cross-tabulations using nominal variables. To display these, use pie and bar charts. Ordinal variables have an implied order between the response choices. Examine the median and mode for the variables and run cross-tabulations or tree-based approaches. Bar charts display the choices well. Interval or continuous variables have an implied order and implied distance between the response options. With variable such as age in years, a one-unit difference is the same throughout the distribution.

These variables lend themselves to a much broader range of powerful statistics than do the previous variable types. Regression analysis is one of the more popular statistical procedures using inter-level variables. Scatterplots and histograms are appropriate graphical displays for these kinds of variables. Try to use continuous variables if appropriate; they will give you more information. Cross-tabulations are appropriate when you have two or more categorical variables. Continuous variables don't lend themselves to cross-tabulation since you would get as many rows or columns as there are different responses. Try to use a t-test to learn about differences in means between groups. You can determine the average age for each group, but you need a procedure like a t-test to confirm if the observed difference is due to chance, or if it can be considered "real." If the significance is less than .05, you will usually conclude that the differences in the observed averages are not due to chance, and that they reflect real population differences.

When presenting the results of a t-test, use a bar chart in which the height of each bar is the average score for each group. If you have more than two groups that you would like to compare, use the ANOVA (Analysis of variance) procedure instead of t-test.

GLOSSARY

analysis of variance: A method of analysis used when dealing with one treatment variable on an interval-scaled dependent variable and one or more nominally-scaled independent variables. A technique to determine if statistically significant differences of means occur between two or more groups.

area sample: A cluster sample in which the primary sample unit is a geographic area

attitude rating scale: Measures used to rate attitudes. Example: the Likert Scale.

Artificial Intelligence (AI): It is a modern technology where computers can mimic patterns, several tasks, and think like human beings. It deals with the simulation of intelligent behavior in computers.

big data: Big data is extremely large data sets that may be analyzed computationally to real patterns, trends, and associations especially relating to human behavior and interactions.

back translation: The process of translating a questionnaire into another language and then back into original language to discover inconsistent meanings

bar chart: A graphic aid that shows changes in a variable at discrete intervals bivariate data analysis: Data analysis and hypothesis testing when the investigation concerns simultaneous investigation of two variables using tests of differences or measures of association between two variables at a time

chi-square test: A test that statistically determines significance in the analysis of frequency distribution. A test statistic often used in crosstabulations to test the hypothesis that the row and column variables are independent. That is, it measures whether the observed distribution is likely due to chance.

cloud computing: A general term used to describe Internet services such as social networking services, online backup services, and applications that run within a web browser. It also includes computer networks that are connected over the Internet for server redundancy or cluster computing purpose.

cluster sampling: An economically efficient sampling technique in which the primary sampling unit is not the individual element in the population, but a large cluster element

coding: The process of identifying and classifying each answer with a numerical score or other character symbol

correlation coefficient: A statistical measure of the covariation of or association between two variables

crosstabulation: A technique organizing data by groups, categories, or classes, thus facilitating comparisons; a joint frequency distribution of observations on two or more sets of variables

cybersecurity: Includes store, manipulation/movement of data networks and devices connected to all IT networks. All these have to be secured against intrusion, unauthorized use, vandalism, identify threat.

database: A collection of raw data or information arranged in a logical manner and organized in a form that can be stored and processed by a computer.

deep learning: It is also known as deep neuron networks (DNN). It is a type of Artificial Intelligence (AI) and is machine-learning technique that enables automatic learning through the absorption of data such as text, images, videos. It is a class of machine learning algorithms that uses multiple layers to progressively extract higher level features from the raw input.

drone: Unmanned aerial vehicle (UAV) with ground-based controller and a system of communication between the two

editing: The process of making data ready for coding and transfer to data storage. Its purpose is to ensure completeness, consistencies, and reliability of data.

error checking: The final stage of the coding process during which codes are verified and corrected as necessary.

exploratory research: Initial research conducted to clarify and define the problem

fact finding: A secondary data study designed to collect descriptive information to support decision-making

follow-up: A letter/postcard/email reminder requesting that a respondent return/email the questionnaire

frequency distribution: Organizing a set of data by summarizing the number of times a particular value of a variable occurs

global digital economy: An economy based on digital computing technologies—Internet/social media

hypothesis: An unproven proposition or supposition that tentatively explains certain facts or phenomena; a proposition that is empirically testable

inferential statistics: Statistics used to make inferences or judgements about a population on the basis of a sample

instrument: A data collection form such as a questionnaire, or other measuring device

Internet: A worldwide network of computers that gives an individual access to information and documents from distant sources

interpretation: The process of making pertinent inferences and drawing conclusions concerning the meaning and implications of a research investigation

interviewer bias: Bias in the responses of subjects due to the influence of the interviewer

Likert scale: A measure of attitudes ranging from very positive to very negative designed to allow respondents to indicate how strongly they agree or disagree with carefully constructed statements relative to an attitudinal object

market research: An activity of systematic gathering information about consumers'/customers' needs and preferences

marketing research: Systematic gathering, recording, and analyzing of qualitative and quantitative data about issues relating to marketing products/services

mean: A measurement of central tendency; the arithmetic average

median: A measure of central tendency that is the midpoint, the value below which half the values in a sample fall

meritocratic system: Is a system in which economic goods/services and political influence are vested in individual people on the basis of intellectual/talent/effort/achievement rather than wealth or social class

mode: A measure of central tendency; the value that occurs most often

monocratic system: A form of system in which the ruler of a country is an absolute dictator—dictatorship/one-man rule/authoritarian

multivariate analysis of variance: (MANOVA). A statistical technique that provides a simultaneous significance test of mean difference between groups, made for two or more dependent variables.

multivariate data analysis: Statistical methods that allow the simultaneous investigation of more than two variables

normal distribution: A symmetrical bell-shaped distribution that describes the expected probability distribution of many chance occurrences

online survey: It is an Internet survey where a set of survey questions is sent out to a target sample and the member of this sample can respond to the questions via worldwide web/Internet.

open-ended question: A question that poses some problem and asks the respondent to answer in his/her own words

percentage distribution: The organization of a frequency distribution into a table or graph that summarizes percentage values associated with particular values of a variable pie chart: A graphic aid that shows the composition of some total quantity of a particular time; each angle or slice is proportional to its percentage of the whole.

pretest: A pretest is like a rehearsal of the actual survey to be conducted. The purpose of a pretest is to highlight problem and issues in order to better implement the final survey.

quota sampling: A nonprobability sampling procedure that ensures that certain characteristics of a population sample will be represented to the exact extent that the investigator desires

random sampling: A sampling procedure that selects population elements based on chance and therefore ensures a sample that accurately represents the population

regression analysis: A technique that attempts to predict the values of a continuous interval-scaled or ratio-scaled dependent variable from the specific values of the independent variable

reliability: The degree to which measures are free from error and therefore yield consistent results

research design: A master plan specifying the methods and procedures for gathering and analyzing needed information

research methodology: A discussion within the body of a research report of the research design, data gathering methods, sampling techniques, fieldwork procedures, and data analysis efforts

research objective: The purpose of the research in measurable terms; the definition of what the research should accomplish

respondent: The person who answers a survey researcher's questions or the person who provides answers to written questions/ emailed questions/self-administered surveys

response rate: The number of questionnaires returned or completed, divided by the total number of eligible people who were contacted or requested to participate in the survey

robot: A robot is machine designed to execute one or more tasks automatically with speed and precision. It is a combination of mechanical, electrical engineering and computer science/engineering that deals with design, construction and operation.

sample: A portion of a population from which information is collected so as to obtain information and draw conclusions about the total population

scatterplot: A graph of data points based on two variables. One variable defines the horizontal axis, and the other variable defines the vertical axis. Most frequently used for displaying continuous data.

secondary data: Data that has been previously collected

self-administered questionnaire: A questionnaire, such as a mail questionnaire, that is filled in by the respondent rather than an interviewer

social media: It is a form of electronic communication such as websites for social networking and microblogging through users create online communities to share information, ideas, personal messages, and other contents.

standard deviation: A quantitative index of a distribution's spread or variability; the square root of the variance for distribution

stratified sample: Sample which selects respondents according to strata or characteristics of interest. For example, race.

systematic sampling: A random sampling method that is equivalent to a simple random sample

tabulation: The orderly arrangement of data in a frequency table or other summary format

target population: The specific, complete group relevant to the research project

T-test: A univariate hypothesis test using the t-distribution rather than the Z-distribution. It is used when the population standard deviation is unknown, and the sample size is small.

univariate data analysis: Analysis that assesses the statistical significance of a hypothesis about a single variable

web survey: A web-based-survey is the collection of data through a self-administered-electronic set of questions on the web.

Z-test: A univariate hypothesis test using the standardized normal distribution which is the distribution of Z

REFERENCES

Aaker, David A. *Marketing Research*. New York: John Willey & Sons, 2012.

Aaker, David A. *Strategic Market Management*. New York: John Willey & Sons, 2014.

Abrahamson, Mark. *Social Research Methods*. Englewood Cliff, NJ: Prentice Hall, 1983.

Achenbaum, Alvin. "The Future Challenge to Market Research," *Marketing Research* 5, no. 2 (1993).

Afuah, Allan, and Tucci, Christopher L. *Internet Business Models and Strategies*. New York: McGraw-Hill, 2003.

Albaum, Gerald, and Duerr, Edwin. *International Marketing and Export Management*. 7th edition. Harlow, 2011.

Aldrich, Richard J. "Beyond the Vigilant State: Globalization and Intelligence." *Review of International Studies* 35, no. 4 (2009): 889–902.

Allen, Eric, and Fjermestad, Jerry. "E-commerce Marketing Strategies: An Integrated Framework and Analysis," *Logistics Information Management* vol. 14, no. 14 (2011): 14–23.

Amato, Louis, and Wilder, Arnold. "Global Competition and Global Markets: Some Empirical Results," *International Business Review*, 13, no. 3 (2004): 401–416.

Armitage, J. "Strategic Insights," *Marketing Insights* 27, no. 1 (2015): 22–23.

Arnold, David. "Seven Rules of International Distribution," *Harvard Business Review* 78 no. 6 (2000): 131–137.

Bainbridge, William S. *Survey Research: A Computer Assisted Introduction*, Belmont, CA: Wadsworth, 1989.

Barnard, Philip. "Conducting and Coordinating Multi-country Quantitative Studies across Europe." *Journal of Market Research Society* 24 (1982).

Baumgartner, Hans, and Steenkamp, Jan-Benedict, "Response Styles in Marketing Research: A Cross-national Investigation." *Journal of Marketing Research* vol.38, no.2: 143–156.

Bednall, David, and Valos, Michael. "Market Research Effectiveness: The Effects of Organizational Structure, Resource Allocation, and Strategic Type." *Australasian Journal of Market and Social Research* 13 no. 2 (2005): 11–27.

Boyd-Barrett, Oliver. "Cyberspace, Globalization, and Empire." *Global Media and Communication* 2, no.1 (2006): 21–41.

Boyd, Danah, and Crawford, Kate. (2012). "Critical Questions for Big Data," *Information, Communication, and Society*, 15, no. 15 (2012): 662–679.

Bryman, Alan. *Social Research Methods*. Oxford: Oxford University Press, 2001.

Burgess, Robert G. *Field Research: A Source Book and Field Manual*. London: Allan and Unwin, 1982.

Burns, Alvin C., and Bush, Ronald F. *Marketing Research*. 7th edition. Harlow: Pearson, 2014.

Burns, Robert B., Burns, Richard A. *Business Research Methods and Statistics Using SPSS*. Sage Publications Ltd., 2008.

Caffin, Philippe, and Wittink, Dick R. "Commercial Use of Conjoint Analysis: A Survey," *Journal of Marketing*, (1982): 44–53.

Caputo, Anne, (2009). "Making the Complex Simple: For Better Business Decision," *Business Information Review* 26 no. 1 (2009): 28–34.

Clark, Terry, and Knowles, Lynette L. "Global Myopia: Globalization Theory in International Business," *Journal of International Management* 9 (2003): 361–72.

Cateora, Philip R, and Graham, John L. *International Marketing*. New York, NY: Irwin/McGraw-Hill, 1999.

Cateora, Philip R, and Graham, John L. *International Marketing*, New York, NY: McGraw Hill Publications, 2003.

Chaffey, Dave. *E-Business and E-Commerce Management: Strategy, Implementation, and Practice*. Paris: Pearson, 2011.

Chen, Hsinchun, Chiang, Roger H.L., and Storey, Veda C. (2012). "Business Intelligence and Analysis: From Big Data to Big Impact," *MIS Quarterly* 36 no. 4 (2012): 1165–1188.

Chisnall, Peter. *Marketing Research*. Berkshire: McGraw Hill Publications, Berkshire, 1997.

Chisnall, Peter. *Marketing Research*. Maidenhead: McGraw Hill Publications, 2001.

Cohen, Goel. *Technology Transfer: Strategic Management in Developing Countries*. SAGE Publications, 2004.

Converse, Jean M. and Presser, Stanley. *Survey Questions: Handcrafting the Standardized Questionnaire*, Quantitative Applications in Social Sciences no. 63. Beverly Hills: Sage, 1986.

Crimp, Margaret, and Wright, Lentiu. *The Marketing Research Process*. Harlow: Prentice Hall, 1995.

Czinkota, Michael R., and Ronkainen, Illeka A. (1998). *International Marketing*. Orlando, Florida: Dryden Press, 1998.

Czinkota, Michael R. "Take a Shortcut to Global Research," *Marketing news* (1995): 3.

de Sousa Santos, Boaventura. "Globalization." *Theory, Culture, and Society* 23. No 2/3 (2006): 393–99.

Di Pietro, Loredana, and Elenora Pantano. "An Empirical Investigation of Social Network Influence on Consumer Purchasing Decision: The Case of Facebook." *Journal of Direct Data and Digital Marketing Practice* 14 (2012): 18–29.

Duncombe, Richard. "Researching the Impact of Mobile Phones for Development: Concepts, Methods, and Lessons for Practice."

Information Technology for Development 17, no. 4 (2011): 268–88.

Dunning, John H. *Making Globalization Good: The Moral Challenges of Global Capitalism.* New York: Oxford University Press, 2003.

Dwyer, Sean, Mesak, Hani, and Hsu, Maxwell. *Journal of International Marketing* 13, no. 2 (2005).

Marks, Eric A., and Lozano, Bob. *Executive's Guide to Cloud Computing.* John Wiley & Sons, Inc., 2010.

Feinstein, Selwyn. "Computers Replacing Interviewers for Personnel and Marketing Tasks," *Wall Street Journal* (1986): 35.

Ferguson, Rick. "Word of Mouth and Viral Marketing: Taking the Temperature of the Hottest Trends in Marketing," *Journal of Consumer Marketing* 25: 178–182.

Franks, Bill. *The Analytics Revolution: How to Improve Your Business by Making Analytical Operations in the Big Data Era.* Hoboker, NJ: Wiley, 2014.

Glazer, Rashi. "Marketing in an Information-intensive Environment: Strategic Implications of Knowledge as an Asset," *Journal of Marketing* (1991): 1–19.

Gould, M. "International Marketing Strategies," *Research Starters Business* 1 (2017).

Goodyear, Mary. "The Trials, Tribulations, and Success in Doing Qualitative Research in the Developing World," *Marketing Review* 37 (1982).

Gummesson, Evert. *Quantitative Research in Management.* Chartwell-Bratt, 1988.

Gummesson, Evert. *Qualitative Methods in Management Research.* 2nd edition. Thousands Oak, CA: Sage Publications Inc., 2002.

Gunther, Marc. "The World New Economic Landscape," *Fortune* (2010): 105–106.

Gruen, Thomas W., Osmovbekov, Talai, and Czaplewski, Andrew J. (2006). "The Impact of Customer-to-customer Online Know-how Exchange on Customer Value and Loyalty," *Journal of Business Research* 59 no. 4 (2006): 449–456.

Hakin, Catherine. *Research Design: Strategies and Choices in Design of Social Research.* London: Allen and Unwin, 1987.

Hamill, J. "The Internet and International Marketing," *International Marketing Review* 14. No. 5 (1997): 800–23.

Hammersley, Martyn, and Atkinson, Paul. *Ethnography: Principles in Practice*. London: Tavistock, 1983.

Harris, Philip R., and Moran, Robert. *Managing Cultural Differences*. Houston, Texas: Gulf publishers, 1996.

Harris, Lisa, and Charles, Dennis. "Engaging Customers on Facebook: Challenges for e-retailers," *Journal of Consumer Behavior* 10 (2011): 338–346.

Heinonen, Kristina. "Consumer Activity in Social Media: Managerial Approaches to Consumers' Social Media Behavior," *Journal of Consumer Behavior* 10 (2011): 356–364.

Herman, Peter. "Globalization Revisited," *Society and Economy* 32. No. 2 (2010): 255–75.

Hirschman, Elizabeth. "Humanistic Inquiry in Marketing Research: Philosophy, Methods, and Criteria," *Journal of Marketing Research* 23, (1986): 237–49.

Hoefstede, Gurt. *Culture's Consequences: International Differences in Work-related Values*. Beverly Hill, California: Sage Publications, 1998.

Hollensen, Svend. *Global Marketing*. 2nd edition, 2011.

Hollensen, Svend. *Essentials of Global Marketing*. Harlow: Pearson, 2012.

Huland, J., and Chow, Yiu Ho. "Managing Use of Casual Model in Marketing Research: A Review," *International Journal of Research in Marketing* 13 no. 2 (1996): 181–197.

Hutt, Michael D., and Speh, Thomas W. *Business Marketing Management*. Orlando, Florida: The Dryden Press, 1994.

Iacobucci, Dawn, and Churchill, Gilbert A. *Marketing Research: Methodological Foundations*. Ohio: Cengage Learning, 2009.

Jaffe, Eugene D. "The Efficacy of Mail Surveys in Developing Countries: The Case in Israel," *European Research* 10 (1982).

Jameson, Fredric, and Masao, Miyoshi. *The Culture of Globalization*. Durham, North Carolina: Duke University Press, 1998.

Jean-Pierre, Jeannet and Hennessey, Hubert D. (1998). *Global Marketing Strategies*. Houghton Mifflin Co., Boston, MA.

Jobber, David, Mirza, Hafiz, and Wee, Kee. "Incentives and Response-rates to across National Business Surveys: A Logic Model Analysis," *Journal of International Business Studies* 4 (1991): 711–721.

Jones, Sue. (1985). "Depth Interviews," *Applied Quantitative Research*. Gower, Aldershot.

Keegan, Warren J. *Global Marketing Management*. Englewood Cliffs, New Jersey: Prentice Hall, 1989.

Keegan, Warren J. and Schlegelmilch, Bodo. *Global Marketing Management: A European Perspective*. Ashford Colour Press Ltd., Gosport, 2011.

Kellner, Douglas. "Theorizing Globalization," *Sociology Theory* 20, no. 3 (2002): 285–305.

Kidder, Louise H., and Judd, Charles M. *Research Methods in Social Relations*. London: H.R.W., 1986.

Kenna, Peggy, and Sondra, Lucy. (1994). *Business Mexico: A Practical Guide to Understanding Mexicans Business Culture*. Chicago, Illinois: Passport Books, 1994.

Kinnear and Taylor, James. *Marketing Research: An Applied Approach*. New York: McGraw-Hill, 1983.

Kinsey, Joanna. *Marketing in Developing Countries*. Macmillan Education, 1994.

Kirk, J., and Miller, M. L. *Reliability and Validity in Qualitative Research*. Beverly Hills, California: Sage, 1986.

Kotler, Philip, and Keller, Kevin. *Marketing Management*. Upper Saddle River, New Jersey: Prentice Hall, 2011.

Lavrakas, P.K. *Telephone Survey Methods*. Newbury Park, California: Sage, 1987.

Lee, S.M., Hwang, T., and Kim, J. "An Analysis of Diversity in Electronic Commerce Research," *International Journal of Electronic Commerce* 12 no. 1 (2007): 31–67.

Lehmann, Donald, R. *Market Research and Analysis*. Homewood, Illinois, 1985.

Leigh, Thomas W., Mackay, David B., and Summers, John O. "Reliability and Validity of Cojoint Analysis and Self-explicated

Weights: A Comparison," *Journal of Marketing Research* (1984): 456–62.

Leitao, Nuno Carlos. "Economic Growth, Globalization, and Trade," *Managing Research and Practice* 4, no. 3 (2012): 18–24.

Levitt, T. "The Globalization of Markets," *Harvard Business Review* 61 no. 3 (1983): 92–102.

Lin, A., and Chen, N.C. "Cloud Computing as an Innovation: Perception, Attitude, and Adoption," *International Journal of Information Management* 32 no. 6 (2012): 533-540.

Luthans, and Doh, J.P. *International Management.* New York: McGraw-Hill, 2010.

Lynch, Alfred P. "In Search of Global Markets," *Strategy and Leadership* (1996): 40.

Macdonald, Emma, K., Wilson, H.N, and Konus. "A New Too Radically Improves Marketing Research," *Harvard Business Review* (2012): 103–108.

MacElroy, B., Mikucki, J., and McDowell, P. "A Comparison of Quality in Open-end Responses and Response Rates between Web-based and Paper and Pencil Survey Modes," *Journal of Online Research* (2002).

Madely, John. "Globalization," *Appropriate Technology* 36, no.1 (2009): 52–53.

McAfee, A., and Brynjolfsson, E. "Big Data: The Management Revolution," *Harvard Business Review* 90, no. 10 (2012): 60–66.

McAfee, A. "What Every CEO Needs to Know about the Cloud," *Harvard Business Review* 89, no. 11 (2011): 124–132.

McGorry, S.Y. "Measurement in Cross-cultural Environment: Survey Translation Issues," *Qualitative Market Research: An International Journal* 3 no. 2 (2000): 74–81.

Mckenna, R. *Total Access: Giving Customers What They Want in an Anytime, Anywhere World.* Harvard Business School Press, 2003.

Martinez, Ruben O. "Globalization and the Social Sciences," *Social Science Journal* 35, no. 4 (1998): 601–613.

Melewar, T.C., and Smith, Nicholas "The Internet Revolution: Some Global Marketing Implications," *Marketing Intelligence and Planning* vol. 20 no. 2 (2003): 363–369.

Meyer, John W. "Globalization: Theory and Trends," *International Journal of Comparative Sociology* 48, no. 4 (2007): 269–74.

Michael, Saren. "Marketing Empowerment and Exclusion in the Information Age," *Marketing Intelligence and Planning*, vol. 29, no.1 (2011): 39–48.

Miles, N.B., and Huberman, A.M. *Qualitative Data Analysis: A Source Book of New Methods*. London: Sage, 1984.

Mishkin, Frederic S. "Globalization and Financial Development," *Journal of Development Economics* 89, no.2 (2009): 164–169.

Morgan, G., and Smircich, L. "The Case for Qualitative Research," *Academy of Management Review* 5 (1980): 491–500.

Montgomery, David B. "Understanding the Japanese Customers, Competitors, and Collaborators," *Japanese and the World Economy* vol. 3 (1991): 61–91.

Morgan-Thomas, A., and Bridgewater, S. "Internet and Exporting: Determinant of Success in Virtual Export Channels," *International Marketing Review* 21 no. 4 (2004): 393–408.

Norusis, M. *The SPSS Guide to Analysis*. Chicago: SPSS Inc., 1986.

Ohmae, Kenichi. "Managing in a Borderless World," *Harvard Business Review* (1989): 152–61.

Onkvisit, Sak, and Shaw, John J. *International Marketing Analysis and Strategy*. Upper Saddle River, New Jersey, NJ: Prentice Hall, 1997.

Paterson, L. "Online Customer Communities." *Business Information Review* 26 no. 1 (2009): 44–50.

Peterson, Bent, Welch, Lawrence S., and Liesch, Peter. "The Internet and Foreign Market Expansion," *Management International Review* 42 no. 2 (2002): 207–21.

Porter, M.E. "Strategy and the Internet," *Harvard Business Review* 79 (2001): 63–78.

Rothaermel, F.T, Kotha, S., and Steensma, H.K. "International Market Entry by US Internet Firms: An Empirical Analysis of Country Risk, National Culture, and Market Size," *Journal of Management* 32 no. 1 (2006): 56–82.

Sandhusan, L. Richard. *Global Marketing*, Barron's Educational Series. New York: Hauppage, 1994.

Saul, John S. *Development after Globalization: Theory and Practice for the Embattled South in New Imperial Age*. London: Zed Books, 2006.

Schiller, Dan. *Digital Capitalism: Networking the Global Market System*. Cambridge, MA: MIT Press, 1999.

Schiller, Dan. "Defining Globalization," *World Economy* 31, no. 11 (2008): 471–501.

Scholte, Jan Aart. "Defining Globalization," World Economy 31 (2008).

Schultz, D. "Marketing from the Outside In," *Journal of Business Strategy* vol. 14, no. 4 (1993): 28.

Schultz, Markus. "The Values of Global Futures," *Current Sociology* 59, no. 2 (2011): 268–72.

Schuster, Camille, and Copeland, Michael. *Global Business*. Hartcourt Brace & Co., 1996.

Scott, Allen, J., and Storper, Michael. "Regions, Globalization, Development," *Regional Studies* 37, no. 6/7 (2003): 579–605.

Smith, Anthony David. *Towards a Global Culture? In Global Culture Nationalization, Globalization, and Modernity*, London: Sage Publications, 1990.

Sodersten, Bo. *Globalization and the Welfare State*. New York: Palgrave Macmillan, 2004.

Steger, M.B. *Globalization: A Very Short Introduction*. Oxford: Oxford University Press, 2003.

Tassey, Gregory. "Globalization of Technology-Based Growth: The Policy Imperative," *Journal of Technology Transfer* 33, no. 6 (2008): 560–78.

Tausch, Arno. "Globalization and Development: The Relevance of Classical Dependency Theory for the World Today," *International Social Science Journal* 61 (2000): 467–88.

Taylor, S.J., and Bogdan, R. *Introduction to Qualitative Research Methods*. New York: Wiley, 1984.

Taylor, M.J., and England, D. "International Marketing: Navigational Design Issues," *Marketing Intelligence and Planning* vol. 24. no. 1 (2006): 77–78.

Terhanian, G., and Bremer, J. "A Smarter Way of Selecting Respondents for Surveys," *International Journal of Market Research* 26 no. 6 (2012): 751–780.

Tse, D.K, Kam-Hon, Lee, Vertinsky, Ilan, and Wehrung, Donald A. "Does Culture Matter? A Cross Cultural Study of Executives' Choice, Decisiveness, and Risk Assessment in International Marketing," *Journal of Marketing* 52, no. 4 (1988): 81–95.

Turner, Graeme. "Shrinking the Borders: Globalization, Culture, and Belonging," *Culture Politics: An International Journal* 3, no. 1 (2007): 5–20.

Tull, Donald, and Hawkins, D.I. *Arch: Measurement and Method.* New York: Macmillan, 1987.

Usunier, Jean-Claude. *Marketing across Cultures.* Hertfordshire: Prentice-Hall, 1996.

Valerie, Sue M., and Ritter, Lois A. *Conducting Online Surveys.* London: Sage Publications, 2012.

Van Maanen, J. *Qualitative Methodology.* London: Sage, 1983.

Vien, C. L. "The Future of Marketing: Thriving in Digital World," *Journal of Accountancy*, 219 no. 6 (2015): 1–4.

Walker, R. *Applied Qualitative Research.* Gower, Aldershot, 1985.

Wilson, Williams J. "Pitfalls in International Research," *Marketing Review* 37 (1982).

Winters, Lewis, C. "International Psychographics," *Marketing Research* vol. 4 (1992): 48–49.

Yazn, A., Saavas, P, Feng, L. "Cloud Computing Adoption by SMEs in the Northeast of England: A Multi-perspective Framework," *Journal of Enterprise Information Management*, 26 no. 3 (2013): 250–275.

Zigmund, Williams G., Carr, J.C., and Griffin, M. *Business Research Methods.* 2012.

Zigmund, Williams G. *Exploring Market Research.* Fort Worth, Texas: The Ryden Press, 1991.

Internet websites

https://www.itu/en/itu-statistics/documents/facts/ict-facts   figures 2019.pdf.

http://www. Itu.int/en/itu-d/statistics/documents/facts/ict-facts figures 2020.pdf.

https://www.internetworldstats.com.

Pew Research Center. (2015). "Internet Use Over Time." http://www.pewinternet.org/dat-trend/internet-use, order-time/.

Andreasen, S. (2013). "Intelligence by Variety in Big Data World." https://www.columnfiremedia.com/world-items/infographic-intelligence-by-variety.

https://www.statista.com.

INDEX

A

Advanced computing technology 18

Analysis of variance (ANOVA) 129, 130, 133, 141

Artificial Intelligence (AI) 8, 13, 16, 18, 22

Automated Insights (NLG) 9

B

Big data 9, 10, 11, 12, 13, 16, 19, 90

Bing 3, 114

Bitcoin 19, 21

Bivariate statistics 133

Business administration vii

Buying behavior patterns 8

C

Cloud computing ix, xi, 9, 12, 13, 16, 18, 22

Cluster analysis 130, 133

Cluster sampling 102

Conjoint analysis 129

Consumer/customer behavior 22

Consumers' lifestyle xi

Convenience sampling 102

Correlation 127, 132

Crosstabulations 128, 140, 141

Cryptocurrencies 21

Cultural barriers 7

Cultural sensitivity ix, 89, 94

Cultural social facts xii, 31, 38, 39, 41, 42, 44, 46, 47, 49, 50, 52, 54, 55, 56, 58, 59, 61, 62, 64, 66, 68, 69, 71, 72, 74, 75, 77, 79, 80, 81, 82, 83

Cybersecurity 17

D

Data analysis xii, 11, 90, 95, 127, 130

Data coding 128

Data warehouse 11, 13
Decision making 90, 111
Deep learning xi, 14, 15, 21
Deep neural networks (DNN)
   21
Deep Neural Networks (DNN)
   xi, 10, 15
Descriptive statistics 129, 130,
   133
Digital computing technology
   15
Digital global market xi
Digitalization xi, 2, 7, 16, 18,
   19, 21, 23, 90, 94
Drones 9

E

e-business 18
e-commerce 1, 6, 14, 18, 22,
   23, 76
Economic facts 39, 41, 42, 43,
   45, 47, 48, 50, 51, 53, 54,
   56, 57, 59, 60, 62, 63, 65,
   66, 67, 69, 70, 72, 73, 75,
   77, 78, 79, 80, 81, 83
Editing 128, 130
Exploratory research 92

F

Facebook 7, 27, 76
Factor analysis 130, 133
Fiber optic cable 3

G

GDP 31, 37, 39, 41, 42, 44, 45,
   47, 49, 50, 51, 53, 55, 56,
   58, 59, 61, 62, 63, 65, 66,

68, 69, 71, 72, 73, 75, 77,
   78, 79, 80, 81, 83, 89
Global communications 7
Global consumers/customers 7
Global databases 7
Global digital economy vii, ix, x,
   xii, 1, 7, 15, 18, 23, 94
Global digital landscape 2, 4, 6,
   8, 11, 16, 21
Global digital market landscape
   16
Global economy ix, 15, 18, 21,
   90
Globalization xi, 18, 19, 21, 94
Global landscape 20
Global living standard xi, 18, 20
Global marketing ix, xii, 16, 24,
   90, 91, 94
Global marketing management
   25, 89
Global marketing research xii,
   89, 90
Global marketing strategy 90
Global market landscape 2, 94,
   98
Global market/marketing
   research vii, ix, xi, 2, 5, 7, 8,
   12, 13, 21, 24, 25, 30, 91,
   92, 94, 95, 97, 98, 100, 101,
   127, 130, 131, 132
Global market/marketing
   researcher ix, 12
Global market/marketing
   researchers ix, 2, 5, 8, 10,
   12, 13, 23, 24, 25, 30, 90,
   92, 94, 132
Global market/marketing
   research survey 4, 93

Global marketplace xii, 2, 5, 17, 18, 24, 89
Global market research xii, 30
Global population 2, 4, 6, 12, 17, 18, 30
Global trade 7, 16, 18, 20
Google 3, 18, 114
Google analytics 3

I

Instagram 7
Intellectual Property system (IPS) Internet 17
Internet/mobile technology 20, 99
Internet of Things (IoT) 4, 9, 13, 18, 22
Internet/online marketing research survey 93
Internet/online/web survey 134
Internet technology 1

L

LinkedIn 7

M

Mail survey 92, 93, 98, 134, 137, 140
Management vii, x, 5, 8, 11, 13, 21, 25, 53, 64, 89, 91, 127, 131, 132
Market analysis 90
Market categories xii, 24, 25
Market facts ix, xii, 31, 37, 39, 40, 43, 45, 47, 48, 49, 51, 53, 54, 56, 59, 60, 61, 63, 64, 66, 67, 69, 70, 72, 73, 75, 77, 78, 79, 80, 81, 82

Marketing vii, xii, 1, 8, 10
Marketing opportunities x
Marketing research x, xii, 2, 5, 7, 9, 11, 12, 19, 25, 31, 89, 92, 96, 100, 127, 129, 130
Market/marketing research plan x
Market research 30, 52, 89, 122
Market strategy 92
Market survey xii
Market trends ix, 7, 8, 90
Mean 133
Meritocratic system xi, 6, 15, 19, 21, 26, 31, 37, 83, 98
Mobile/smartphone 4, 5, 7, 16, 17, 83, 84
Mobile/smartphone technology 1, 2, 16, 94
Monocratic system 19, 25, 31, 75, 84, 130
Multi-countries x, 91
Multidimensional scaling 130
Multivariate methods 128

N

Natural language processing (NLP) Online surveys 14

O

Online/Internet survey 92, 94

P

Poisson Distribution analysis 133
Primary data 91
Probability sampling 102

Q

Qualitative/quantitative data 89,
    127
Questionnaire xii, 8, 92, 94, 96,
    99, 101, 103, 107, 115, 119,
    122, 126, 134, 137

R

Regression analysis 129, 133,
    141
Research design x, xii, 90, 91,
    100
Respondent 92, 95, 96, 98, 101,
    135, 136, 138

S

Sampling xii, 5, 93, 95, 96, 101,
    134
Satellites 3
Secondary data x, 25, 30, 90, 91
Secondary market research 25
Secondary research 25, 91

Simple random sampling 102
Snowball sampling 102
Social media ix, xi, 2, 6, 8, 16,
    20, 22, 76, 94, 98
Social media networks 8
Statistical package for social
    science (SPSS) 132
Stratified sampling 102
Survey instrument xii, 94, 96,
    97
Survey methods 92, 94
Survey research 93, 96, 99, 132

T

Tabulating data 130
t-tests 129, 133
Twitter 7

U

Univariate statistics 127

ABOUT THE AUTHOR

Author Dan V. Nathan holds an MBA and MSc in marketing management from Plymouth Business School (UK) and University of Glamorgan (South Wales), respectively. He is a member of The Chartered Institute of Marketing, UK, since 1979 after graduating with a postgraduate diploma in marketing. He is currently a fellowship member (FCIM) of the institute. He has four decades of experience working for a group of companies such as Chesebrough-Pond's, EMI, SRC, Neiman Marus, BCBS, and many other reputable companies in marketing, statistics, entrepreneurship, information technology, and customer relationship management. He can be reached at danviv2045@gmail.com.

www.ingramcontent.com/pod-product-compliance
Lightning Source LLC
Chambersburg PA
CBHW021409210526
45463CB00001B/288